Farm to Table cookbook

Farm to Table cookbook

Discover the joys
of local farm fresh food

This edition published in 2013
LOVE FOOD is an imprint of Parragon Books Ltd

Parragon
Chartist House
15–17 Trim Street
Bath, BA1 1HA, UK

Copyright © Parragon Books Ltd 2007

LOVE FOOD and the accompanying heart device is a registered
trademark of Parragon Books Ltd in Australia, the UK, USA, India,
and the EU.

www.parragon.com/lovefood

ISBN: 978-1-4723-1873-2
Printed in China

Produced by Ivy Contract
Photography by Clive Streeter
Home economists: Angela Drake and Teresa Goldfinch

Notes for the Reader
This book uses metric, imperial, and US cup measurements.
Follow the same units of measurements throughout; do not mix
metric and imperial. All spoon and cup measurements are level unless
otherwise indicated. Unless otherwise stated, milk is assumed to be
whole, eggs are large, individual vegetables are medium, and pepper
is freshly ground black pepper. Unless otherwise stated, all root
vegetables should be washed in plain water and peeled prior
to using. For best results, use a food thermometer when cooking
meat and poultry. Check the latest USDA government guidelines
for current advice.

Garnishes, decorations, and serving suggestions are all optional and
not necessarily included in the recipe ingredients or method. The
times given are only an approximate guide. Preparation times differ
according to the techniques used by different people and the cooking
times may also vary from those given. Optional ingredients,variations,
or serving suggestions have not been included in the time
calculations.

Recipes using raw or very lightly cooked eggs should be avoided by
infants, the elderly, pregnant women, convalescents, and anyone with
a weakened immune system. Pregnant and breast-feeding women are
advised to avoid eating peanuts and peanut products. People with
nut allergies should be aware that some of the prepared ingredients
used in the recipes in this book may contain nuts. Always check the
packaging before use. Vegetarians should be aware that some of the
prepared ingredients used in the recipes in this book may contain
animal products. Always check the package before use.

The publisher world like to thank the following for permission to
reproduce copyright material on the cover: Radishes on blue wooden
surface © Studer-T. Veronika/Getty Images.

Contents

Foreword

It doesn't take a genius to work out that you could use just the same recipes for cooking organic ingredients as you would for nonorganic. But what better time could there be to review your kitchen repertoire, than when you start to include organic produce in your weekly shopping basket? The Organic Seasonal Cookbook brings a new and clear vision of what's possible when you tread the organic path. Liz Franklin's recipes are inspiring, urging us toward the freshest, brightest, most delectable ways to use the extraordinary range of organic ingredients to which we now have ready access. Embracing both the reassuringly familiar and the latest trends (fennel fritters ride high on my list of recipes to try), organic eating has rarely seemed more interesting and inviting.

How times change. Just a couple of decades ago, organic food was treated as something of a joke. Well, to be honest it was hard to find and when you did finally stumble across a wholefood store housing a clutch of baskets half-full of organic apples, potatoes, and carrots, all too often they looked tired and dusty and past their prime. You had to be dedicated to pay up for such miserable offerings. No wonder the rest of the nation's shoppers laughed scornfully.

Who's laughing now? Not only those original brave pioneers, but so many more of us who have leapt aboard this most optimistic of movements. Organic farming and production methods offer a beam of hope in a world that sometimes seems all too beset with disaster. Here's a brilliant success story in which we can all play a small part. Slip a copy of The Organic Seasonal Cookbook under your arm, and let Liz show you the way.

Sophie Grigson

Introduction

In the course of our busy, time-pressured lives, many of us have unwittingly become creatures of habit. We eat similar foods all year round, taking for granted their constant availability, and often not taking into account the distance they may have traveled to reach our plates and the intervention needed to keep them in optimum condition. We now know that for our own personal health and that of our planet, we need to slow down, reconnect with the seasons, and live more sustainable lives. Going organic is the natural way to redress the balance and tune in to the changing rhythms of the seasons, so that life becomes healthier and happier.

Food, farming, and well-being

We all know that nourishment of the body and soul is essential to human survival; without food and water, we would die. Since food is the product of agriculture, the integrity of our farming practices must undoubtedly be linked to the well-being of our bodies. The paradox of the present day is that intensive-farming methods, pesticides, and drugs that were introduced in order to improve the quality of our food can, in some ways, have the opposite effect.

The manufacture and development of synthetic fertilizers has made for easier crop cultivation, and the use of antibiotics and vitamin supplements in animal nutrition has meant that certain breeds of livestock can be raised indoors and in large numbers—often more quickly than nature might originally have intended. Also, the massive developments made in transportation and technology mean that we can circumnavigate the globe with speed. For generations, our diets were largely influenced by the seasons: fresh strawberries or pods of sweet, newly picked peas were an eagerly awaited summer treat, fall would herald the orchard harvest, and hearty roots to be baked and mashed were a sure sign that winter was on its way. Now we can air freight them around the globe all year round, and in the developed world we have grown accustomed to having every season's fare at our fingertips.

But on the downside, the incidence of obesity and diet-related diseases is on the increase, food scares make headline news on a regular basis, and one-sixth of the world's farmable land has been lost to soil degradation caused by intensive cultivation.

Steps toward sustainability

It isn't only comestibles that we take for granted. We have power at the push of a button and water at the turn of a tap; we jump in our cars for the shortest of journeys and jet off on holiday to far-flung destinations with little thought for the environmental impact.

However, by thinking a little more carefully about the relationship between planet and plate, and making some easily achievable changes to the way we shop and eat, we can redress the balance. Buying seasonal, organically produced food, choosing fish from sustainable sources, conserving energy consumption, and curbing waste are simple steps we can all take to reawaken our taste buds, sharpen our appreciation of the environment in which we live, and lead healthier, more contented lives, as well as leave the world in better shape for future generations.

Farming the organic way

Organic farming is about sound environmental management. Emphasis is placed on soil health through crop rotation and the application of natural manures and composts. Crop rotation is based on age-old farming methods. Crops are not grown in the same place year after year, but "alternated" so that they are not returned to the same site for at least three years. This discourages soil-borne pests and diseases that cause soil erosion, and improves soil fertility and structure. The use of pesticides and fertilizers is heavily restricted.

Animal welfare is a priority, with greater living space and access to outdoors a prerequisite. The routine administration of antibiotics and medicines to accelerate growth and prevent disease is not permitted. Organic farming practices create crops and animals that are inherently robust, enabling them to develop a natural resistance to disease.

Tastier, healthier food

Most people who eat organic food do so because they find that it tastes nicer than conventionally farmed food. By and large, organic fruit and vegetables grow at a slower rate than their conventionally raised counterparts. They ripen naturally and often have a lower water content too, which can play a role in achieving a fuller, truer flavor. In the case of meat, organically raised animals are given the freedom to forage, graze and exercise; this makes the meat leaner and denser, with an improved flavor and texture.

Research has shown that overall, organically grown fruit and vegetables are richer in vitamin C and essential minerals than non-organically grown specimens. Organic milk has a naturally higher omega-3 fatty acid content than non-organic milk.

Organic food doesn't contain many of the additives that are allowed in non-organic food such as hydrogenated fats, aspartame (the artificial sweetener), and monosodium glutamate, all of which have been linked with health problems such as asthma and heart disease. In addition, some food additives have been associated with unwanted conditions such as allergic reactions and hyperactivity.

Exposure to potentially harmful pesticides is avoided; over 440 pesticides can be recurrently used in non-organic farming and residues are often found in non-organic food.

Antibiotic resistance in humans is a rising problem; there have been links to additives routinely added to animal food in order to accelerate animal growth. Organic standards disallow the regular use of antibiotics.

Organic criteria do not allow for the use of genetically modified (GM) crops or ingredients. In order to achieve organic status, all organic farms and food companies are inspected annually and have to meet exacting legislatory standards. In this way, consumers can be sure that the food that they eat has grown in the way that nature intended.

Happier animals and a healthier ecosystem

Animals are inherently happier when raised within the bounds of organic animal husbandry, with its strict welfare standards. For example, studies have shown organic milk contains considerably more vitamin E and beta-carotene than non-organic milk. This is because the diet of organically raised cows is much more natural than that of intensively raised animals—their diet is based on freshly grazed grass and clover, whereas for the most part, non-organic cows eat a largely grain-based diet that contains cereals and protein supplements. The production of grain and protein supplements in turn requires more intensive farming, and so the cycle continues.

Taken as a whole, organic farming creates less chemical pollution, produces lower amounts of carbon dioxide, and, generally speaking, better supports farmland wildlife than nonorganic farming. Habitat management encourages the use of field margins such as hedges, trees, and grass or herbaceous strips, which break up excessively large blocks of crops that have a tendency to be more vulnerable to disease and pest outbreaks. This in turn promotes biodiversity, which is crucial for a healthy ecosystem.

Rediscovering the seasons

Of the many easily achievable—as well as hugely enjoyable—contributions to organic living we can make, perhaps the first is to rediscover and work with the rhythm of the seasons in the way we shop for food and plan our meals. Our hectic lifestyles may mean we have to shop in the most time-effective, convenient way, but many of our grocery stores and supermarkets are becoming increasingly environmentally aware and now stock locally sourced and ethically produced goods and ingredients. We can also supplement our shopping by using farmers' markets or, where possible, vegetable box schemes, and buying direct from small producers. Some of us might discover hidden gardening talents by planting a tub or two of herbs, a small patch of potatoes, or a few rows of carrots at home, which can be highly therapeutic and rewarding.

We can all find ourselves trapped in a routine with our meal planning; when we have busy lives, it is all too easy to fill our shopping trolleys with similar items week in and week out, serving the same basic repertoire of dishes over and over again. By using the changing seasons as a benchmark for our buying and cooking, we are naturally encouraged to experiment and be a little more inventive, and in doing so we are likely to discover new favorites. Mealtimes become special again, rather than just being a rushed affair simply for the purpose of refueling.

Seasonal eating ensures you are consuming what is naturally good for you at the right time of year. It also benefits local producers and cuts down on the amount of food miles. Those who are interested in the quality of food and are aware when certain ingredients are at their best will naturally end up eating more of the foods in season and less of those flown halfway around the globe. But ultimately, eating seasonally is all about enjoying food, rather than abstinence.

Making more out of a meal

It is an irony that in our modern-day lives we seem to have more conveniences and yet less time. At the end of a hectic week, we can often find it difficult to remember what we actually did with it. We all need to eat on the run from time to time, but even after a busy day, a little time spent in the kitchen can be more therapeutic than we realize, and a meal shared with friends and family incredibly restorative for the soul.

Cooking up something tasty for dinner does not mean that we have to be confined to the kitchen for hours. It is possible to have a pot of enticing food bubbling away on the hob while you take a shower, or have a mouthwatering roast in the oven while you catch up with your emails or vacuum the floor. And if fast food is a necessity, it need not be full of preservatives or encased in packaging—how long does it take to boil a simple bowl of pasta, then drizzle over some olive oil and grate over a little Parmesan cheese?

Preserving pleasures

Some of the most delicious meals imaginable have been born out of thrift, to use up leftovers or make the most of a glut of fresh fruit or vegetables. For example, many of the Italian food favorites that we have all grown to love so much around the world are rooted in *cucina povera*, the peasant or rural cookery that made the most of natural ingredients available such as bread, fruit, vegetables, grains, and olive oil. Indeed, bread has always been a fundamental part of the Italian diet and was never wasted, but how many of us now would turn the last piece into breadcrumbs to thicken a sauce or cut it up and bake it into crisp golden croutons? Likewise, who among us would think to buy a chicken to provide one meal and use its carcass to make a stock or soup that will form the basis of another? And few of us nowadays would consider buying extra vegetables or fruit to take home and make into chutney or jelly, and yet the techniques for preserving that we still use today arose from our need to store valuable foodstuffs harvested during times of abundance for the leaner periods.

From ancient times, all around the globe, cultures have experimented with food preservation methods. In order to live, it was necessary to extend the shelf life of the foodstuffs at hand, as there was never enough fresh food to eat all the year round. Over the centuries, more sophisticated ways to pot and pickle, dry, salt, and smoke have developed; not only fruit and vegetables, but meat and fish. Next time you eat a slice of ham or smoked salmon, remember that these foods came about because in the past what we ate was linked so closely to the seasons.

While few of us have the time or the inclination to cure our own meats or smoke our own fish, we can reap the benefits of a return to working with the seasons and buying as much food as possible closer to home.

Seasonal delights

The fact that we have changing seasons should make us recognize the value of them more; while some of us may dream of summer all year round, wrapping up for crisp winter walks can also be enjoyable in its own way. Likewise, the fact that some foodstuffs have short availability should be the very reason that makes them so special. Asparagus is a prime example; its wonderful flavor is best appreciated soon out of the ground. The home-grown season may be short, but why not eat it at its most glorious, looking to other delights when the harvest is over, while eagerly anticipating its arrival again the following year? As the spring turns into summer, we can then move on to savoring crisp green beans or sweet young carrots in their prime. Choosing what is in season and looks good on the day can make shopping much more fun and meals far more exciting.

Seasonal food is fresher and tends to be tastier and more nutritious. By relying a little less on pre-packaged foods and more on natural, homemade meals made from fresh ingredients, we are also taking steps toward a healthier lifestyle and diet. Instead of quickly consuming a takeaway meal or snacking on convenience foods in front of the television, a little exercise in the form of chopping and stirring could make all the difference, and provide us with a more nutritious, satisfying, and enjoyable eating experience too.

Changing the way we shop and eat needn't be hard work. Building a nourishing diet and making the most of fresh produce can be a lot easier than we may have let ourselves believe in recent times. A good basic pantry that includes spices and seasonings, olive oil, rice, beans, flour, and maybe a can or two of tomatoes will make a valuable and versatile foundation. Then simply build your menus around what fresh ingredients are best for the time of year.

Focus on the type of dish and cooking method rather than following a recipe in every detail; that way you can adapt and adjust to whatever is available. If you don't have pumpkin for your pie, for example, try sweet potato instead, or if you can't find carrots for your cake, grate in a parsnip or two. And if your basil is looking limp, replace it with some lively parsley.

In this way, you can experiment in your cooking and use the recipes in this book as a guide, so feel free to swap and substitute ingredients; only with baking do you need to be a little more precise.

Reduce, reuse, and recycle

Our throwaway lifestyle is having an alarming effect on the planet's natural resources. Reducing the amount of waste we produce is vital; it saves on essential raw materials and reduces energy production, too. Reusing items can make a big difference. Carrier bags are a prime example; don't throw them away but keep using them over and over again. Taking unwanted clothes, toys, and furniture to charity shops means that other people can benefit; there are even organizations that can make use of old spectacles, computers, and cell phones, for example.

Recycling can also have a massive impact on the war on waste. Every tonne of paper that is recycled saves 17 trees, and 36 gallons/136 liters of oil are saved for every tonne of glass that is recycled. Aluminum cans may be recycled indefinitely, conserving raw materials and reducing by 95 percent the energy needed to create new ones. Plastic takes centuries to break down, so be aware of biodegradable packaging and use less plastic packaging.

When shopping, try to purchase goods that are made to last and that you know are definitely recyclable. When buying wood for decorating projects, buy reclaimed or recycled wood, or buy lumber that comes from trees that are not under threat. Do the same with furniture, too.

Kitchen and garden waste can be used to make organic compost, helping to preserve valuable peat bogs. All that is needed is a sturdy bin and a sunny site. Quick-rotting waste such as fruit and vegetable peelings, tea bags, grass, and plant cuttings will provide nitrogen and moisture, while eggshells will add minerals. Egg boxes, screwed-up paper, and fallen leaves provide fiber and carbon, and help to form air pockets in the mixture that will encourage decay. In this way, you have your own easy recipe for nutrient-rich mulch that will help to beautify your garden and assist in lightening your trash can.

Carbon footprints and offsetting

A carbon footprint is a measure of the impact that day-to-day human activities have on the environment in relation to the amount of greenhouse gases generated, calculated in units of carbon dioxide or CO_2. Carbon offsetting involves paying a commercial organization to reduce or counterbalance an individual's greenhouse gas emissions, through various schemes that invest in renewable energy, such as wind or solar power, and forest planting projects. The idea is to calculate your carbon footprint, and pay a suitable amount toward a project that compensates for it.

Simple ways of reducing CO_2 emissions include walking and cycling instead of driving, joining car share schemes, and driving at lower speeds to reduce fuel consumption. At home, switch appliances off that aren't being used and switch to energy-efficient lighting and appliances. Make sure that your home is well insulated, and turn down the heating a degree or two. Even little things like showering rather than taking a bath and turning the tap off when brushing your teeth can help. And, eat locally produced and seasonal food—using the lovely recipes from this book—to cut down on air miles.

Fair Trade

Shopping seasonally and locally should be something we prioritize, but tropical fruits can provide an occasional treat and coffee and tea are consumed by most of us. Many of these goods originate from poor countries. Fair Trade is an organization that contributes to sustainable development by promoting sound environmental practices. They aim to secure fair prices and offer improved trading conditions to small producers and disadvantaged workers. Although not all Fair Trade products are organic, there are many shared values between the organic movement and Fair Trade.

Spring

Vegetables

artichokes	fava beans	radishes
asparagus (late spring)	fennel	scallions
	kale	shallots
beets (except late spring)	leeks	snow peas
cabbage (all green varieties)	mushrooms (white, cremini, portobello)	sorrel
carrots		spinach
cauliflower	mustard greens	squash
celeriac	onion (red, white, salad)	sugar snap peas
chives		swede
collard greens	potatoes	watercress

Fish and Seafood

salmon (wild)	whitebait
sea trout (late spring)	

Fruit

apples (cooking, baking)	mango	strawberries
apricots	pineapple	
avocado	rhubarb	

Meat, Poultry, and Game

beef	lamb (spring)	venison (all year, but particularly winter)
chicken	pork	
duck	quail	
guinea fowl	rabbit	

Summer

Vegetables

artichokes (globe)	cauliflower (except early summer)	peas
arugula		potatoes
asparagus (early summer)	corn	radicchio
	cucumber	radishes
beans (string, round, flat, fava, green)	eggplants	scallions
	fennel	shallots
beets	kohlrabi	snow peas
bell peppers (all varieties)	lettuce	sorrel
	mushrooms (white, cremini, portobello)	spinach
broccoli		Swiss chard
cabbage (all green varieties)	onion (red, white, salad)	tomatoes
		turnips
carrots	parsley	watercress
		zucchini

Fish and Seafood

crab	mackerel	sea trout
crayfish	sardines	shrimp
herring	sea bream	squid
lobster	scallops	whitebait

Fruit

blackberries	nectarines	raspberries
blueberries	peaches	watermelon
cherries	plums (late summer)	

Meat, Poultry, and Game

beef	grouse (late summer)	quail
chicken		rabbit
duck	guinea fowl	venison (all year, but particularly winter)
goose	lamb	
	pork	

Fall

Vegetables

artichokes (globe)

artichokes (Jerusalem, late autumn)

arugula

beets

borlotti beans (fresh)

broccoli

cabbage (all green varieties)

carrots

cauliflower

corn (early autumn)

cucumber

endive

garlic

kohlrabi

lettuce

mushrooms (white, cremini, portabello)

onion (red, white, salad)

parsley

parsnips

potatoes

pumpkins

radicchio

radishes

scallions

shallots

sorrel

spinach

squash

sweet potatoes

Swiss chard

tomatoes

turnips

wild mushrooms

zucchini

Fish and Seafood

lobster

mackerel

shrimp

sardines

sea trout (early autumn)

squid

Fruit

apples (early eating)

figs

ginger

grapes

nectarines

peaches

plums

pears (late autumn)

pomegranate

raspberries

Meat, Poultry, and Game

beef

chicken

duck

goose

grouse

guinea fowl

hare

lamb

partridge

pheasant

pigeon

pork

quail

rabbit

venison

Winter

Vegetables

artichokes (Jerusalem)

arugula

beets

Brussels sprouts

cabbage (all green varieties)

cabbage (red)

carrots

cauliflower

celeriac

celery

endives

kale

leeks

mushrooms (white, cremini, portabello)

onion (red, white, salad)

parsnips

potatoes

radicchio

radishes

rutabaga

scallions

shallots

squash

sweet potatoes

turnips

Fish and Seafood

oysters

Fruit

apples (cooking, baking)

chestnuts

grapefruit

oranges

rhubarb

Meat, Poultry, and Game

beef

chicken

duck

goose

guinea fowl

grouse

hare

lamb

partridge

pheasant

pigeon

venison

Spring

Spring starts in a flurry of wet, blustery days and yet draws to a close beneath a mantle of spring flowers. There is an infectious optimism in the air as the days grow progressively warmer and our daily dose of sunlight increases. At long last, all our thermal gear can be safely stored away, and mealtimes and menus become a lighter affair. The slow-cooked warming meals that have sustained us through the cold winter days and dark evenings can now be replaced with refreshingly simple dishes.

After its long winter hibernation, the ground may still be a little drowsy at first; in early spring, the soil can struggle to produce an impressive array of fresh vegetables or a brimming fruit bowl, but as the season moves on, there are some real treats in store.

Easter is the focus for this season's celebrations, and many of us will have at least some of the time earmarked for extra entertaining. Chocoholics can enjoy a little guilt-free indulgence and Easter egg hunts delight the children. Now is the time to enjoy the new season's lamb, and an elegant crown of lamb or a leg roasted to pink perfection will make a handsome centerpiece for a special gathering. Despite the all-year-round availability of potatoes, spring's tiny and tasty new crop make an especially delicious combination with lamb.

Tender shoots of kale, dark green mustard greens, and creamy white cauliflowers are ripe for discovery. Leeks can be used as an alternative to onions in cooked dishes or served as a side dish. Conical spring cabbages are ready in the garden, crisp and light green, and delicious lightly cooked or served raw in salads. Chives, sorrel, and mint are the first herbs to produce soft, usable leaves in the spring, adding fresh flavors to soups and egg and potato dishes.

By the tail end of the season, the orchards are in blossom and the first young spears of fresh local asparagus are appearing—a delicacy not to be missed. The chubby, tender shoots are perfect when lightly cooked and have a great affinity with eggs and creamy dressings.

Given a slick of olive oil, a scattering of salt, and a short roasting, the lovely flavors of asparagus are enhanced. The longer, less-robust, and thinner spears (known as sprue) are ideal for sauces, soups, and tarts.

Summer

The summer months are abundant with good things to eat. School is out, the weekends seem to last longer, and we often feel much more sociable. Warm, sunny days and long, light evenings were made for fuss-free alfresco dining, and the simplest after-work supper eaten out of doors can melt away memories of a difficult day almost instantly.

Newly picked asparagus and luscious local strawberries have to be early summer's heroes. We have grown accustomed to seeing strawberries all year round, but often at the sacrifice of flavor. A bowl of sun-ripened strawberries, grown on home ground and simply served with a little cream and a dusting of sugar, is one of this season's finest pleasures.

Juicy, plump cherries are wonderful eaten unadorned straight from the bag, or serve them with fresh new season goat cheese for the easiest of treats. Alternatively, try baking them into a delicious tart with dense, almond frangipane and buttery, crisp pastry. There are so many other soft fruits available in summer we are spoiled for choice—from succulent blackberries and jewel-like blueberries to plump, perfumed nectarines and apricots.

Top-quality ingredients need just the gentlest nudge of outside intervention and should form the heart of summer eating. It is the prime time for native lettuce varieties—the sweet and crunchy Boston lettuce is undoubtedly a joy just now, and cool, crisp romaine types have good flavor, too. Fava beans are in full swing, young zucchini are blooming, and midsummer brings the chance to pick your own peas.

Globe artichokes now flourish, as do scallions and cucumbers. As summer progresses, tomatoes, string and green beans, bell peppers, and eggplants are ready. Summer squash and the first root vegetables also appear.

Herbs are plentiful and many can be frozen—chop them or leave them whole to pep up dishes, such as soups and casseroles, in the bleaker months.

Although some may regard fish as being fiddly to prepare, it does make great real fast food. Salmon and trout are available now and suit a delicate approach, but light up the barbecue to bring out the best in oily sardines and mackerel. Crab is an outstanding substantial shellfish, while shrimp and whitebait make choice little nibbles.

Fall

Bright and sunny September days may offer hints of an Indian summer, but the month's fresher mornings and tell-tale carpets of burnished bronze leaves are a sure sign that fall has indeed arrived.

In the kitchen, the pace is slowing down. Long, delicious braises and casseroles replace summer's speedy salads and grills. From beets to blackberries and pumpkins to pears, falll brings us warming roots, succulent orchard fruits, and, for some of us if we are fortunate enough, a free feast from the bushes.

Pumpkins are plentiful now; all too often they are used simply as decorative lanterns for Halloween celebrations, but they are wonderful oven-baked and coaxed to delectable life with garlic and pungent spices. Game foods are abundant—grouse, guinea fowl, pheasant, and partridge can all grace the table, accompanied by tubers and roots such as Jerusalem artichokes, turnips, carrots, and kohlrabi. Nuts such as crisp, fresh-tasting, milky hazelnuts as well as walnuts can also be found.

In early fall, grapes, plums, and blueberries will still be available, and there are late-season raspberries and juicy blackberries to enjoy. Now is the time to pull out the preserving pan and start pickling and potting to make the most of early fall's glut of vegetables and stone fruits. Preserves, jellies, and chutneys will all perk up plates through the cooler months and offer a tasty reminder of warmer days.

Down in the forest, fungi foragers are on the trail of the most exquisite wild food. Porcini, the so-called mushroom kings, should be around now, with their white flesh and deep nutty flavor; delicious served in simple creamy sauces or stir-fried.

As winter draws near, temperatures fall considerably and thoughts turn to fireside feasts and sturdier fare for snacking too. Toasted treats, cakes, and mugs of warming hot chocolate are perennial favorites.

With the run-up to Christmas, November brings cheery food vendors to street corners with the unmistakable aroma of roasting chestnuts wafting on the air. Now is the time when the more organized among us begin culinary preparations for the festive season.

Winter

Cold, crisp days and long, dark evenings signal that winter has arrived. We yearn for filling, wholesome foods that satisfy and soothe us through the dismal, damp, and chilly weather conditions. Comforting, leisurely simmered stews, rich roasts, and hearty soups form the mainstay of the season's meals and the quick-cooking grill pan and broiler now give way to the casserole and crock pot.

Although winter appears to be the season with the least to offer in terms of locally grown produce, take a closer look and you will discover many delights to sample. Root vegetables really come into their own in winter. All roots can be roasted and mashed to concentrate their robust flavors, while celeriac, parsnips, and potatoes in particular bake down beautifully in creamy gratins. Sweet potatoes make silky smooth soups and are at their best baked in their skins and topped with good butter, maybe with a crown of crispy bacon.

Bold-flavored brassicas are a characteristic winter feature. The splendid, crinkly-textured savoy is the king of the cabbages, and tender young sprouts are delicious.

Fruit options are limited, although apples and pears last well into the winter months. Citrus fruits are at their best now. Typically high in vitamin C, they are full of goodness and can help to boost your winter immune system and fight off colds. Make use of dried fruits such as raisins and dates, to add richness and sweetness to baked dishes and desserts as well as to savory salads.

To satisfy carnivorous cravings, beef is a good choice. Hogget is lamb just under a year old, and ideal for slow cooking and for marrying with stronger flavors. For faster food, gutsy flavored game birds suit the earlier winter months, although by the turn of the year their toughened flesh is better suited to robust casseroles and stews. The fattier birds such as duck and goose are especially good for holiday entertaining.

January is the month when many of us attempt to repent the excesses of the festive season. Low fat venison or poultry and crunchy winter salads can be a great recourse. It is a good time to seek inspiration from the pantry and spice rack to enliven jaded palates, so turn up the heat a notch or two with an occasional curry or chili.

Spring

Spring brings a sense of anticipation and an increase in energy levels, making it the ideal time to start experimenting with the first of the year's crops. Winter roots are replaced with crisp green leaves and newly-picked herbs, including chives and mint, resulting in naturally lighter dishes and refreshing sauces and dressings. Try serving chilled soups and no-bake cookies, and replace the comforting desserts of winter with fresh fruit such as rhubarb.

Sun-dried Tomato Sauce with Spring Vegetables

Serves 4

1 lb 12 oz/800 g prepared mixed spring vegetables, especially celery stalks, asparagus spears, broccoli florets, and artichoke hearts

country-style bread, cut into bite-size cubes, toasted if preferred

Sauce

generous ¾ cup extra virgin olive oil

3 garlic cloves, thinly sliced

1¾ oz/50 g canned anchovy fillets in olive oil, drained

1 tbsp unsalted butter (optional)

3–4 sun-dried tomatoes in oil, drained and very finely chopped

4–5 fresh basil leaves, torn

A tasty version of the classic warm Italian sauce known as bagna cauda, which includes sun-dried tomatoes for extra pizzazz.

1 Lightly cook vegetables such as asparagus and artichoke hearts (and broccoli, if preferred) separately in boiling water until just tender. Drain and let cool.

2 Arrange on a pretty plate with the other vegetables and the bread cubes. Alternatively, serve the bread cubes in a separate little basket or dish.

3 To make the sauce, put the oil, garlic, and anchovies in a saucepan over very low heat. Mash the anchovies with a fork and heat, stirring, for 3–4 minutes, or until they have started to melt into the oil and the garlic slices have softened. Take care not to let the mixture become too hot, or the garlic will simply fry and the mixture will be spoiled. Stir in the butter, if using, and sun-dried tomatoes.

4 Transfer the mixture to a small serving bowl and stir in the basil. Serve immediately with the prepared vegetables and bread cubes.

Little Scallion, Pea, and Ricotta Tarts

Simply flavored ricotta makes a light but tasty filling for these crisp little tarts.

1 To make the pastry, sift the flour and salt together into a bowl or food processor, then add the butter and rub in with your fingertips or process until the mixture resembles fine breadcrumbs. Add the egg and enough cold water to form a smooth dough. Cover and refrigerate for 30 minutes.

2 Preheat the oven to 375°F/190°C. Lightly grease a deep, 12-cup muffin pan.

3 Roll the pastry out on a floured work surface to a thickness of about ½ inch/3–4 mm. Using a round pastry cutter or glass, cut out rounds large enough to line the cups of the muffin pan. Gently press the pastry shells into the cups. Line each pastry shell with a small piece of parchment paper and fill with dried beans.

4 Bake the pastry shells in the preheated oven for 4–5 minutes, or until golden and crisp. Remove the paper and beans.

5 Meanwhile, to make the filling, mix the ricotta and Pecorino cheeses together in a large bowl. Add the egg, scallions, and peas. Chop the peppercorns very finely, then add to the mixture. Season to taste with salt and a good grinding of pepper.

6 Spoon the filling into the pastry shells and bake for 10 minutes, or until golden. Serve warm.

Makes 12

Pastry

1⅓ cups all-purpose flour, plus extra for dusting

pinch of salt

1⅛ sticks butter, diced, plus extra for greasing

1 egg yolk

Filling

9 oz/250 g ricotta cheese

3½ oz/100 g Pecorino cheese

1 egg, beaten

12 scallions, finely chopped

2 tbsp fresh shelled peas, lightly cooked and cooled

1 tsp green peppercorns in brine, drained

salt and pepper

Broccoli, Chile, and Garlic Crostini

Serves 6

1 lb 2 oz/500 g broccoli, stems trimmed and cut into lengths short enough to fit on the crostini

scant ½ cup olive oil

1 small clove garlic, chopped

1–2 red chiles, seeded and finely chopped

6 slices good-quality country-style bread

salt and pepper

Crostini are small, thin slices of toasted bread, which are usually served brushed with olive oil. In this recipe, broccoli and chile are combined to create a nutritious crostini with a kick!

1 Preheat the oven to 375°F/190°C .

2 Cook the broccoli in a large saucepan of salted water for 10 minutes, or until just tender. Drain well and set aside.

3 Heat about one-third of the oil in a wok or large skillet over high heat, then add the garlic and chile and stir-fry for 2 minutes. Add the broccoli, then season to taste with salt and pepper and stir-fry for 3–4 minutes, or until hot and crisp.

4 Meanwhile, drizzle the remaining oil evenly over the bread slices and bake in the preheated oven for 10 minutes, or until crisp and golden.

5 Divide the broccoli mixture between the crostini, add a grinding of pepper, and serve immediately.

Butter has a great affinity with asparagus—a seasonal treat that should not be missed.

1 Preheat the oven to 400°F/200°C.

2 Lay the asparagus spears out in a single layer on a large baking sheet. Drizzle over the oil, then season to taste with salt and pepper and roast in the preheated oven for 10 minutes, or until just tender.

3 Meanwhile, make the sauce. Pour the lemon juice into a saucepan and add the water. Heat for a minute or so, then slowly add the butter, cube by cube, stirring constantly until it has all been incorporated. Season to taste with pepper and serve immediately with the asparagus.

Asparagus with Lemon Butter Sauce

Serves 4

1 lb 12 oz/800 g asparagus spears, trimmed

1 tbsp olive oil

salt and pepper

Sauce

juice of ½ lemon

2 tbsp water

⅞ stick butter, cut into cubes

Pasta with Honeyed Chicory and Toasted Walnuts

Serves 4

3 tbsp olive oil

2 garlic cloves, crushed

3 heads chicory, sliced

1 tbsp runny honey

1 cup walnuts

1 lb/450 g dried penne pasta

salt and pepper

Honey complements the slightly bitter taste of chicory, which makes a lovely combination with toasted walnuts and pasta.

1 Heat the oil in a skillet over low heat, then add the garlic and chicory and cook, stirring, for 3–4 minutes, or until the chicory begins to wilt. Stir in the honey and walnuts and cook, stirring occasionally, for an additional 4–5 minutes. Season to taste with salt and pepper.

2 Meanwhile, cook the pasta in a large saucepan of lightly salted boiling water according to the package directions, or until al dente. Drain and toss with the chicory mixture. Serve immediately.

Cook's Tip

You can scatter over a little grated Parmesan cheese to serve, if you like.

Lemon Butter Leeks with Poor Man's Parmesan

For centuries, crisp sautéed crumbs of ciabatta have been commonly used in certain regions of Italy as the poor man's substitute for Parmesan cheese. They actually make a worthy and wonderful topping for all manner of dishes; here, for lemony, buttered leeks with little puddles of melted mascarpone.

1 Preheat the oven to 375°F/190°C.

2 Lay the halved leeks out in an even layer in an ovenproof dish. Drizzle over the lemon juice and scatter over the lemon rind, then sprinkle the sugar evenly over. Season to taste with pepper and evenly dot with the butter. Bake in the preheated oven for 15 minutes, or until the leeks are beginning to soften and caramelize.

3 Meanwhile, make the Poor Man's Parmesan. Melt the butter in a skillet over medium heat, then add the ciabatta crumbs and cook, stirring, until crisp and golden. Season with a little salt and pepper and set aside.

4 Remove the leeks from the oven and evenly dot with the mascarpone cheese. Scatter the Poor Man's Parmesan over the leeks and return to the oven. Bake for an additional 5 minutes, or until the mascarpone has melted and the crumbs are hot and crisp. Serve immediately.

Serves 6

9 chubby leeks, trimmed and halved lengthwise

juice and finely grated rind of 1 unwaxed lemon

1 tsp superfine sugar

scant 3 tbsp butter

5 tbsp mascarpone cheese

salt and pepper

Poor Man's Parmesan

2 tbsp butter

1 cup fresh ciabatta crumbs

Salmon with Warm Preserved Lemon and Black Olive Dressing

Serves 4

2 tbsp olive oil

4 salmon fillets, skin on, about 6 oz/175 g each

juice of ½ lemon

salt

Black Olive Dressing

1 handful fresh basil leaves

2 tbsp snipped fresh chives

1 garlic clove, crushed

1 tsp whole grain mustard

½ tsp superfine sugar

juice of ½ lemon

generous ¾ cup extra virgin olive oil

rind of ½ preserved lemon, finely chopped

10 pitted black olives, finely chopped

A recipe that's simplicity itself. Organic salmon has a far better flavor and texture than farmed salmon, and is a much more environmentally friendly choice. Serve with buttery new potatoes.

1 Preheat the oven to 400°F/200°C.

2 To make the dressing, put the herbs, garlic, mustard, sugar, lemon juice, and extra virgin olive oil in a blender or food processor and whiz until smooth. Pour the mixture into a small saucepan, then add the preserved lemon rind and olives and warm over gentle heat.

3 Meanwhile, heat the olive oil in a skillet over medium heat, then add the salmon fillets, skin-side down, and cook for 3 minutes, or until the skin is golden and crisp. Lay the fish in a roasting pan, skin-side up, then squeeze over the lemon juice and season with a little salt.

4 Roast in the preheated oven for 5 minutes, or until the fish is just cooked through—the exact timing will depend on the thickness of the fillets. Serve immediately with the dressing.

3 tbsp olive oil

1 onion, sliced

3½ oz/100 g pancetta lardons

1 spring cabbage, shredded

1–2 tsp juniper berries, lightly crushed

salt and pepper

Stir-fried Spring Cabbage with Juniper and Pancetta

This is an ideal dish to accompany roast meats and poultry, but delicate enough to complement fish too, especially the oily varieties, such as salmon.

1 Heat the oil in a wok or large skillet over medium-high heat, then add the onion and cook, stirring, for 3–4 minutes, or until softened but not colored. Add the pancetta lardons and cook, stirring, for 3–4 minutes, or until cooked.

2 Meanwhile, lightly steam the cabbage.

3 Add the steamed cabbage and juniper berries to the wok or skillet and stir-fry for 3–4 minutes, or until softened and glistening. Season to taste with salt and pepper and serve immediately.

Peppered Lamb Chops with Onion and Gorgonzola Gratin

The gratin is seriously addictive, and makes a great accompaniment to any roast meat.

1 Preheat the oven to 350°F/180°C. Lightly grease a gratin dish.

2 Lay the onions out in an even layer in the prepared gratin dish. Pour over the sherry, then scatter over the thyme leaves and season to taste with salt and pepper. Dot the mascarpone cheese evenly over the onions and scatter with the Gorgonzola cheese. Bake in the preheated oven for 30–40 minutes, or until the onions are soft and the gratin is golden and bubbling.

3 Meanwhile, brush the lamb with 1 tablespoon of the oil and season with a little salt. Roll in the ground peppercorns. Heat the remaining oil in a skillet over high heat, then add the lamb chops and cook for 3–4 minutes on each side. Let rest for 5 minutes, then slice and serve immediately with the onion gratin.

Cook's Tip
Roast potatoes and dark green vegetables make a perfect accompaniment.

Serves 4

2 lb/900 g lamb chops

3 tbsp olive oil

2–3 tbsp black peppercorns, coarsely ground

Onion Gratin

butter, for greasing

6 onions, sliced

3–4 tbsp dry sherry or white wine

1 tbsp fresh thyme leaves

3–4 tbsp mascarpone cheese

5 oz/150 g Gorgonzola cheese, crumbled

salt and pepper

Creamed Morels on Spinach and Cornmeal Croutons

Morels and cream are a marriage made in heaven. Spooned over crisp cornmeal croutons, they make a special course for a vegetarian dinner party, but will equally delight fervent carnivores.

1 To make the cornmeal, bring the stock to a rolling boil and add the cornmeal in a steady stream, stirring quickly with a large balloon whisk. Cook according to the package directions. When the cornmeal is cooked, switch to a wooden spoon and stir in the Parmesan cheese, spinach, peppercorns, and half the butter. Taste and adjust the seasoning, if necessary.

2 Pour the cornmeal mixture out onto a lightly oiled baking sheet, then smooth over with a palette knife and let cool. When the cornmeal has set, use a 4-inch/10-cm round pastry cutter to cut out the required number of rounds.

3 Cut the morels in half and gently wash them, taking care to remove any traces of soil and grit. Dry gently with kitchen paper. Heat the oil in a saucepan over medium heat, then add the shallots and garlic and cook for 3–4 minutes, or until softened. Add the morels and cook, stirring constantly, for 2 minutes. Pour in the Marsala and bubble briefly, then add the cream, mustard, and tarragon. Season to taste with salt and pepper. Keep warm.

4 Heat the remaining butter in a skillet over high heat, then add the cornmeal croutons and cook for 3–4 minutes on each side, or until crisp and golden. Serve immediately, heaped with the creamed morels and garnished with tarragon.

Cook's Tips
Take care to wash the morels thoroughly—soil and grit can be notoriously difficult to dislodge—but do it just before cooking, or both flavor and texture may be compromised. Unless you have time on your hands and a hankering for big biceps, use one of the brands of quick-cook cornmeal now readily available.

Serves 4–6

6 handfuls fresh morels

3 tbsp olive oil

4 shallots, finely chopped

2 garlic cloves, crushed

scant ½ cup Marsala

generous ¾ cup heavy cream

2 tbsp whole grain mustard

1 small bunch fresh tarragon, finely chopped, plus extra for garnish

salt and pepper

Cornmeal Croutons

4 cups well-flavored vegetable stock

9 oz/250 g cornmeal

1 cup freshly grated Parmesan cheese

2 handfuls baby spinach, coarsely torn

2 tsp coarsely cracked black peppercorns

⅞ stick butter, softened

olive oil, for oiling

Orange and Almond Tart

Serves 6

Pastry

1½ sticks salted butter, softened

¼ cup superfine sugar

1 egg yolk

1½ cups all-purpose flour, sifted, plus extra for dusting

Filling

1 unwaxed orange

1⅛ sticks butter

1 cup superfine sugar

2 eggs, beaten

generous 1 cup ground almonds

Adding a whole puréed orange gives this tart a gorgeously intense orange flavor. Serve with cold pouring cream, vanilla ice cream, or even chocolate sherbet.

1 To make the pastry, beat the butter and sugar together in a bowl until light and fluffy. Add the egg yolk and stir until fully incorporated and smooth. Gradually add the flour and mix until the dough forms a ball, taking care not to overwork. Divide in half and freeze one half. Wrap the remaining pastry in plastic wrap and let rest at room temperature for 20 minutes or so.

2 Roll the pastry out on a floured work surface and use to line an 8-inch/20-cm tart pan with a removable base. Refrigerate until required.

3 Preheat the oven to 350°F/180°C.

4 To make the filling, put the orange into a microwave-proof bowl and add a little water to the bowl. Cover with plastic wrap and cook in a microwave oven for 6–8 minutes on High until the orange is completely soft. Alternatively, put the orange in a saucepan, then cover with water and simmer for 40 minutes, or until completely soft. Let the softened orange cool slightly, then cut in half and remove the seeds. Put in a food processor and whiz to a purée. Add the butter, sugar, eggs, and almonds and whiz again until smooth.

5 Spoon the mixture into the tart base and bake in the preheated oven for 40 minutes, or until the filling is firm. Remove from the oven and let cool. Serve the tart in slices.

Cook's Tip
The pastry recipe yields enough for two tarts, but contains one egg yolk and so is impractical to make less. Simply freeze half and you have pastry ready for next time!

Makes 12

9 oz/250 g rhubarb

1⅛ sticks butter, melted and cooled

scant ½ cup milk

2 eggs, beaten

1⅓ cups all-purpose flour

2 tsp baking powder

generous ½ cup superfine sugar

3 tbsp raisins

3 pieces preserved ginger, chopped

Rhubarb, Ginger, and Raisin Muffins

With a lovely tang of fresh, fruity rhubarb, these muffins also make a lovely treat for breakfast served with yogurt.

1 Preheat the oven to 375°F/190°C. Line a 12-cup muffin pan with paper muffin cases.

2 Chop the rhubarb into lengths of about ½ inch/1 cm. Pour the melted butter and milk into a large bowl and beat in the eggs. Sift the flour and baking powder together and lightly fold into the wet mixture, together with the sugar. Gently stir in the rhubarb, raisins, and preserved ginger.

3 Spoon the mixture into the muffin cases and bake in the preheated oven for 15–20 minutes, or until the muffins are risen and golden and spring back when gently touched in the center with the tip of a finger. Serve warm.

Banana and Brown Sugar Ripple Desserts with Roasted Pecans

Serves 4

⅓ cup pecans

1 tsp superfine sugar

1 lb 10 oz/750 g Greek-style yogurt

3 tbsp dark brown sugar

3 ripe bananas

This recipe is great for using up ripe bananas. Roasting the pecans with sugar really brings out their flavor.

1 Preheat the oven to 375°F/190°C.

2 Toss the pecans in the superfine sugar, then scatter over a baking sheet and roast in the preheated oven for 4–5 minutes, or until golden. Remove from the oven and let cool, then coarsely chop.

3 Spoon the yogurt into a large bowl and sprinkle the dark brown sugar evenly over the top. Let stand for 5 minutes, or until the sugar begins to melt, and then fold it very lightly into the yogurt to create a rippled effect.

4 Peel and slice the bananas, then divide between four pretty dessert glasses. Carefully spoon the yogurt over, taking care to retain the rippled effect. Top with a scattering of the roasted pecans and serve immediately.

Cook's Tip

For a rich flavor and creamy consistency, make sure that you use whole yogurt for this recipe.

Flambéed Pineapple with Little Coconut Cakes

This recipe works beautifully with plums, pears, bananas, or apples. Simply adapt the liqueur accordingly—for example, Calvados is fantastic with apples, dark rum with bananas, and so on.

1 Preheat the oven to 325°F/160°C. Lightly grease a baking sheet.

2 To make the coconut cakes, put the coconut in a large bowl and stir in the sugar and melted butter until evenly mixed. Add the egg and stir well. Form the mixture into small pyramids—this is easiest to do using a small dariole mold or even a shot glass. Put the cakes onto the prepared baking sheet and cook in the preheated oven for 15 minutes, or until golden. Transfer to a wire rack and let cool.

3 Melt the butter in a preheated wok or skillet over high heat, then add the pineapple and cook, stirring frequently, for 4–5 minutes. Stir in the sugar and cook for an adddditional 3–4 minutes, or until the pineapple is softened and buttery but not mushy. Add the rum and set alight.

4 As soon as the flames have died down, serve the pineapple with a good dollop of ice cream or sour cream, if desired, and the little coconut cakes.

Serves 6

scant ½ stick butter

1 ripe pineapple, peeled, cored, and cut into chunks or slices

½ cup superfine sugar

3–4 tbsp rum or coconut liqueur

ice cream or sour cream, for serving (optional)

Coconut Cakes

7 oz/200 g dry unsweetened coconut

¼ cup oz superfine sugar

scant ½ stick butter, melted and cooled, plus extra for greasing

1 egg, beaten

Hot Apple Fritters with Nutmeg Ice Cream

Serves 6

⅓ cup all-purpose flour

generous ⅓ cup cornstarch

pinch of salt

1 tsp baking powder

1 egg

⅔ cup iced water

5 tart eating apples, cored and sliced

olive or sunflower oil, for deep-frying

superfine sugar, for dusting

Nutmeg Ice cream

1 cup heavy cream

generous ¾ cup whole milk

4 egg yolks

generous ½ cup superfine sugar

pinch of salt

freshly grated nutmeg, to taste

Nutmeg ice cream makes a wonderful accompaniment to crisp apple fritters cooked in a tempura-style batter.

1 To make the ice cream, put the cream and milk in a saucepan and heat until almost boiling. Whisk the egg yolks, sugar, and salt together in a bowl. Pour the hot cream mixture into the egg yolk mixture and stir well. Pass the mixture through a fine sieve. Add a little nutmeg to taste, then stir well and let cool. Transfer to an ice cream machine and churn according to the manufacturer's directions until frozen. Alternatively, pour the mixture into a freezerproof container and freeze until almost solid. Remove from the freezer and beat until smooth to prevent the formation of ice crystals. Return to the freezer and freeze until solid. Remove from the freezer 10–15 minutes before serving, to soften a little.

2 Meanwhile, sift the flour, cornstarch, salt, and baking powder together into a large bowl. Stir in the egg and water and mix to a fairly smooth batter.

3 Heat the oil in a deep-fat fryer to 350–375°F/180–190°C, or until a cube of bread browns in 30 seconds. Dip the apple slices into the batter, then add to the hot oil and cook until crisp and golden. Remove with a slotted spoon and drain on paper towels.

4 Dust the apple fritters with superfine sugar and serve immediately with the ice cream.

Summer

Summer is perhaps the best time for seasonal cooking because the range of fresh fruits and vegetables is enormous and most of them require only the minimum amount of effort to prepare. Summer fruits and vegetables have a high water content and are quenching and cooling—just what is needed on hot, sunny days. Rather than spend time in the kitchen, now is your chance to create delicious cooling salads, lightly stir-fried vegetables, and picnic food that can be easily made in advance.

Salt Chili Squid with Watercress and Baby Spinach Salad

Fresh from the sea, this succulent, chili-spiked squid dish makes a great addition to a summer barbecue party.

1 To make the dressing, mix all the ingredients together in a bowl, season with salt and pepper to taste, then cover and refrigerate until required.

2 Cut the squid tubes into 2-inch/5-cm pieces, then score diamond patterns lightly across the flesh with the tip of a sharp knife. Heat the oil in a wok or large skillet over high heat, then add the squid pieces and tentacles and stir-fry for 1 minute. Add the chiles and scallions and stir-fry for an additional minute. Season to taste with salt and pepper and add a good squeeze of lemon juice.

3 Mix the watercress and spinach together, then toss with enough of the dressing to coat lightly. Serve immediately with the squid, together with lemon wedges to squeeze over the squid.

Serves 4

12 squid tubes and tentacles (about 1 lb 9 oz/700 g total weight), cleaned and prepared

2–3 tbsp olive oil

1–2 red chiles, seeded and thinly sliced

2 scallions, finely chopped

lemon wedges, for squeezing and for serving

3 good handfuls watercress

2 handfuls baby spinach or arugula

salt and pepper

Dressing

scant ½ cup olive oil

juice of 1 lime

1 tsp superfine sugar

2 shallots, thinly sliced

1 tomato, peeled, seeded, and finely chopped

1 garlic clove, crushed

Quick Chicken Laksa

This makes an easy starter to a Thai-style meal or an almost instant standby supper.

1 Pour the coconut milk and stock into a saucepan and stir in the laksa paste. Add the chicken strips and simmer for 10–15 minutes over gentle heat, or until the chicken is cooked through.

2 Stir in the tomatoes, sugar snap peas, and noodles. Simmer for an additional 2–3 minutes. Stir in the cilantro and serve immediately.

Cook's Tip
Laksa paste is available from larger supermarkets and Asian stores.

Serves 4

3¾ cups canned coconut milk

generous ¾ cup chicken stock

2–3 tbsp laksa paste

3 skinless, boneless chicken breasts, about 6 oz/175 g each, sliced into strips

9 oz/250 g cherry tomatoes, halved

9 oz/250 g sugar snap peas, diagonally halved

7 oz/200 g dried rice noodles

1 bunch fresh cilantro, coarsely chopped

Crumbed Fennel Fritters with Spiced Bell Pepper Mayo

Serves 6

3 fennel bulbs, trimmed

2 cups stale white breadcrumbs

3½ oz/100 g Parmesan cheese

2 tsp fennel seeds (optional)

1 egg, beaten

sunflower oil, for frying

salt and pepper

lemon wedges, for serving

Spiced Bell Pepper Mayo

2 red bell peppers

1 egg

1 tsp Dijon mustard

2–3 tbsp white wine vinegar

pinch of salt

1¼ cups sunflower oil

2 red chiles, seeded and chopped

Slices of fennel coated in cheesy crumbs and fried until golden make a lovely starter or vegetable accompaniment, and even work as a vegetarian main course. They are great with roasted tomatoes too.

1 For the mayo, using tongs, carefully hold each red bell pepper in turn over a high gas flame, turning frequently, for 8–10 minutes, or until blackened all over. Alternatively, preheat the oven to 425°F/220°C. Put the bell peppers on a baking sheet and cook in the preheated oven, turning frequently, for 10–15 minutes, or until blackened all over.

2 Put the bell peppers in a plastic bag, then seal and let cool. Peel off the charred skins and remove the seeds.

3 Put the egg, mustard, vinegar, and salt in a blender and whiz to combine. With the motor running, slowly trickle in about one-third of the oil. Once the mixture starts to thicken, add the remaining oil more quickly. When all the oil is incorporated, add the chiles and roasted bell peppers and whiz until smooth. Stir in a good grinding of pepper, then cover and refrigerate until required.

4 Cook the fennel bulbs in a large saucepan of salted boiling water for 15 minutes, or until almost tender—the exact cooking time will depend on their size. Drain and let cool, then carefully slice.

5 Mix the breadcrumbs and Parmesan cheese together, then stir in the fennel seeds, if using, and season to taste with salt and pepper. Transfer the breadcrumb mixture to a large plate. Put the egg in a shallow dish. Coat the fennel slices in the egg and press the breadcrumb mixture firmly onto both sides.

6 Cover the bottom of a large skillet with oil to a depth of ½ inch/1 cm. Heat over medium heat, then add the fennel slices and cook, turning once, until golden brown. Remove and drain on paper towels. Serve immediately with lemon wedges to squeeze over and the Spiced Bell Pepper Mayo.

Lobster and Summer Herb Salad with Saffron Mayonnaise

This makes a lovely summer lunch or supper, and can be also served as a luxurious starter.

1 For the mayonnaise, soak the saffron threads in a little warm water. Meanwhile, put the egg, mustard, vinegar, and salt in a blender and whiz to combine. With the motor running, slowly trickle in about one-third of the sunflower oil. Once the mixture starts to thicken, add the remaining oil more quickly. When all the oil has been incorporated, add the saffron and its soaking water and whiz to combine. Add more salt and pepper, to taste, then cover and refrigerate until required.

2 Put the lobster meat and avocado in a bowl. Quarter the tomatoes and remove the seeds. Cut the flesh into fairly chunky dice and add to the bowl. Season the lobster mixture to taste with salt and pepper and gently stir in enough of the mayonnaise to give everything a light coating.

3 Toss the salad greens with the olive oil and lemon juice. Divide between four plates and top with the lobster mixture. Serve immediately.

Serves 4–6

1 lb 10 oz–1 lb 12 oz/750–800g freshly cooked lobster meat, cut into bite-size chunks

1 large avocado, peeled, pitted, and cut into chunky dice

4 ripe but firm tomatoes

9 oz/250 g mixed herb salad greens

1–2 tbsp fruity olive oil

squeeze of lemon juice

salt and pepper

Saffron Mayonnaise

pinch of saffron threads

1 egg

1 tsp Dijon mustard

1 tbsp white wine vinegar

pinch of salt

1¼ cups sunflower oil

Barbecued Beef Skewers with Butternut Panzanella

Panzanella can often be a stodgy disappointment if dominated by soggy, oil-soaked bread. Here, crisp chunks of ciabatta are used which, combined with sweet roasted butternut squash and all the other goodies, makes a fabulous salad to go with juicy barbecued beef skewers.

Serves 4–6

4 fillet steaks, about 5½ oz/ 150 g each

2–3 tbsp olive oil

salt and pepper

Butternut Panzanella

2 butternut squash

⅔ cup extra virgin olive oil

1 stale ciabatta loaf

2 celery stalks, sliced

1 red onion, halved and thinly sliced

1 red bell pepper, seeded and cut into thin strips

9 oz/250 g baby plum tomatoes, halved

12 canned anchovy fillets in olive oil, rinsed and chopped (optional)

1 small cucumber

3 tbsp red wine vinegar

2 garlic cloves, crushed

1 bunch fresh basil, coarsely torn

sea salt flakes

1 Preheat the oven to 400°F/200°C. Presoak 16–20 wooden skewers in cold water for 30 minutes.

2 First make the panzanella. Peel the squash, then remove the seeds and reserve. Cut the flesh into ¾-inch/2-cm chunks and spread out in a roasting pan. Remove any stringy flesh from the seeds, then add the seeds to the squash chunks. Drizzle over a little of the extra virgin olive oil and add a light scattering of sea salt flakes. Roast in the preheated oven for 25 minutes, or until soft and caramelized.

3 Meanwhile, cut the ciabatta into small chunks, then drizzle with some of the remaining oil and season to taste with sea salt flakes. Bake in the oven for 10 minutes, or until golden and crunchy.

4 Put the celery, onion, red bell pepper, tomatoes, and anchovies, if using, in a large bowl. Halve the cucumber lengthwise and scoop out the seeds, then cut into thin slices and add to the bowl. Add the roasted squash and seeds and the baked ciabatta. Mix the vinegar and garlic with the remaining oil and season to taste with salt and pepper. Pour over the salad, then add the basil and toss thoroughly, making sure that the ciabatta chunks get a good coating of the dressing. If possible, let stand for an hour or so to enable the flavors to develop and the bread to soften very slightly.

5 Preheat a broiler or gas barbecue to high, or prepare a charcoal barbecue. Cut the steaks lengthwise into ribbons about ½ inch/1 cm wide. Thread onto the skewers, then brush with the olive oil and season to taste with salt and pepper. Broil or barbecue to your liking—1 minute or so on each side for rare, 2 minutes for medium, and until blackened for well done!

Zucchini Flower Fritters

Serves 4–6

²⁄₃ **cup self-rising flour**

1 tsp baking powder

1 tbsp extra virgin olive oil

1 egg, beaten

generous ¾–1 cup iced water

olive oil, for frying

16–20 zucchini blossoms

salt and pepper

sea salt flakes

lemon wedges, for serving

Delicate zucchini blossoms fried in feather-light batter have to be one of summer's true edible delights.

1 Sift the flour and baking powder together into a bowl and add the extra virgin olive oil and egg. Stir in enough of the water to make a batter with the consistency of heavy cream (the exact quantity may vary according to the flour used). Season to taste with salt and a little pepper.

2 Pour a shallow layer of olive oil into a large skillet or wok and heat over high heat until very hot. Dip the zucchini blossoms briefly in the batter, then add to the oil and cook, in batches, for 2–4 minutes, or until crisp and golden. Remove with a slotted spoon and drain on paper towels. Serve immediately, lightly sprinkled with sea salt flakes and with lemon wedges for squeezing over.

Serves 4–6

1 lb 2 oz/500 g fine green beans

1 lb 2 oz/500 g strawberries

2–3 tbsp pistachios

1 small bunch fresh mint leaves

1 lb 2 oz/500 g feta cheese
(drained weight)

salt and pepper

Dressing

2 tbsp raspberry vinegar

2 tsp superfine sugar

1 tbsp Dijon mustard

pinch of salt

½ cup olive oil

Feta, Mint, and Strawberry Salad with Green Beans and Pistachios

Juicy summer strawberries make a mouthwatering combination with fresh mint and salty feta cheese.

1 To make the dressing, mix the vinegar, sugar, mustard, and salt together in a bowl until smooth. Slowly pour in the oil, whisking constantly until the mixture has emulsified. Cover and refrigerate until required.

2 Blanch the beans in a large saucepan of salted boiling water for 1–2 minutes, so that they retain plenty of crunch. Drain and quickly toss in a large, cool bowl. Hull and halve the strawberries, then add to the beans. Stir in the pistachios and mint leaves. Toss the salad with enough of the dressing to coat lightly.

3 Break the feta cheese into chunks and scatter over the salad. Add a good grinding of pepper and serve immediately.

Cook's Tip
Be generous with the pepper—and be sure to make it coarsely ground.

Variation
Strawberry or red wine vinegars both make great substitutes for the raspberry vinegar.

Spaghetti with Fresh Pea Pesto and Fava Beans

Serves 4

9 oz/250 g shelled fava beans

1 lb 2 oz/500 g dried spaghetti

salt and pepper

Pea Pesto

3 cups fresh shelled peas

5 tbsp extra virgin olive oil

2 garlic cloves, crushed

3½ oz/100 g Parmesan cheese, freshly grated, plus extra, shaved, for serving

⅔ cup blanched almonds, chopped

pinch of sugar

Fresh peas and milky almonds make the most delicious pesto, while fava beans provide the perfect accompaniment. Peeling the fava beans to remove the dull outer skins takes time, but the result is definitely worth it.

1 For the pesto, cook the peas in a saucepan of boiling water for 2–3 minutes, or until just tender. Drain and transfer to a blender or food processor. Add the oil, garlic, and Parmesan cheese and process to a coarse paste. Add the almonds and process again. Add the sugar and season to taste with salt and pepper. Set aside.

2 Blanch the fava beans in a saucepan of salted boiling water until just tender. Drain and let cool. Peel off the dull skins.

3 Cook the spaghetti in a large saucepan of lightly salted boiling water according to the package directions, or until al dente. Drain, then stir in the fava beans and toss with the pesto. Add a good coarse grinding of pepper and serve immediately with shavings of Parmesan cheese.

Sea Bream with Fennel and Tomato Butter Sauce

Serves 4

4 sea bream fillets, skin on, about 6 oz/175 g each

2 tbsp olive oil

salt and pepper

fresh parsley, for garnish

Baked Fennel

4 fennel bulbs, trimmed

1 tbsp superfine sugar

juice of ½ lemon

6 tbsp olive oil

2–3 tbsp pastis (optional)

Tomato Butter Sauce

8 large vine-ripened tomatoes

1 tbsp extra virgin olive oil

1 tbsp good-quality tomato ketchup

scant ¾ stick butter, cut into cubes

This makes a lovely main course for a special summer dinner party. Serve with buttery new potatoes.

1 Preheat the oven to 400°F/200°C.

2 For the baked fennel, slice the fennel bulbs lengthwise and put in a casserole. Sprinkle with the sugar and lemon juice. Season to taste with salt and pepper and pour over the olive oil. Cover with foil and bake in the preheated oven for 30 minutes, or until tender. Remove from the oven, then pour over the pastis, if using, and return to the oven, uncovered, for an additional 10 minutes. If you are not using the pastis, simply uncover and return to the oven.

3 Meanwhile, to make the sauce, put the tomatoes in a food processor and whiz to a purée. Pass through a sieve into a medium saucepan. Heat gently, then stir in the extra virgin olive oil and tomato ketchup. Set aside.

4 Brush the fish fillets with a little of the olive oil and season lightly with salt and pepper. Heat the remaining oil in an ovenproof skillet over medium-high heat, then add the fish fillets, skin-side down, and cook for 1 minute. Turn the fillets over and cook for an additional minute. Transfer to the oven and cook for 2–3 minutes.

5 Just before serving, gently reheat the sauce and whisk in the butter, cube by cube, until fully incorporated. Season to taste with salt and pepper.

6 Divide the fennel between four warmed plates and top each with a fish fillet. Spoon the sauce around and serve immediately, garnished with parsley.

Summer Vegetable and Herb Quiche

Serves 4–6

2 red bell peppers

4 tbsp olive oil

12 oz/350 g puff pastry, thawed if frozen

all-purpose flour, for dusting

2 ripe but firm tomatoes, thinly sliced

9 oz/250 g ricotta cheese

1 cup grated Parmesan cheese

1 tsp fresh thyme leaves

1 tbsp finely snipped fresh chives

salt and pepper

Made with puff pastry, this lovely tart is quick and easy to make, and never fails to delight!

1 Preheat the oven to 400°F/200°C.

2 Remove the stalks and seeds from the bell peppers, and cut the flesh into thin strips. Transfer to a baking sheet and drizzle with half the oil. Season to taste with salt and pepper and roast in the preheated oven for 20 minutes, or until soft. Remove from the oven and let cool while you prepare the quiche shell.

3 Roll the pastry out on a floured work surface and use to line a 9-inch/23-cm tart pan. Prick the base with a fork to prevent the pastry from puffing up.

4 Scatter the roasted bell peppers evenly over the base, then arrange the tomato slices on top and season to taste with salt and pepper.

5 Beat the ricotta cheese in a bowl until smooth, then spoon over the vegetables. Sprinkle over the Parmesan cheese, thyme leaves, and chives, then drizzle over the remaining oil. Bake in the preheated oven for 20 minutes, or until the pastry and cheese topping are golden. Serve immediately, or let cool.

Serves 6

1 lb 2 oz/500 g mascarpone

**generous ½ cup superfine sugar, plus
2 tbsp, or to taste**

1 vanilla bean

½ cup heavy cream

scant ¼ cup crème de cassis

1 lb 2 oz/500 g blackberries

Little Soft Cheese Hearts with Blackberries

Summer berries and mascarpone have a special affinity, as you will see if you try this refreshing and healthy summer dessert.

1 Line 6 Coeur à la Crème molds with butter cheesecloth.

2 Spoon the mascarpone into a large bowl and add the generous ½ cup sugar. Slit the vanilla bean lengthwise with a sharp knife and scrape the seeds into the bowl. Stir well until the mixture is very smooth.

3 In a separate bowl, whip the cream until it forms soft peaks, then fold into the mascarpone mixture. Spoon the mixture into the prepared molds, then tap hard on a work surface to level and set the molds on a tray to catch any whey that runs from them. Refrigerate for several hours—preferably overnight.

4 Pour the crème de cassis over the blackberries 30 minutes before serving and add the remaining sugar, to taste.

5 To serve, simply turn the hearts out of the molds onto individual plates and serve with the blackberries.

Cook's Tip
You can buy Coeur à la Crème molds from good kitchen stores and department stores.

4 egg yolks

¼ cup superfine sugar

½ cup orange Muscat dessert wine

6 ripe but firm peaches

Fresh Peaches with Orange Zabaglione

Soft summer peaches and Muscat wine make a heavenly combination for a special dinner party.

1 To make the sabayon, put the egg yolks, sugar, and wine in a large heatproof bowl over a saucepan of gently simmering water. Using a hand-held electric whisk, whisk for 10 minutes, or until very pale and thick. The bowl should never become so hot that you can't touch it comfortably—if the mixture overheats, you may well end up with a bowl of sweet scrambled eggs! When the mixture is ready, the whisk should leave ribbon trails when lifted. Remove from the heat.

2 Preheat the broiler to high. Cut the peaches in half and remove the pits. Slice the flesh thinly and arrange over a pretty, flameproof plate.

3 Pour the sabayon over the peaches and cook under the preheated broiler for 1–2 minutes, or until the zabaglione is a beautiful golden brown. Serve immediately.

Apricot and Rosemary Clafoutis

This dessert is delicious served warm with a good vanilla ice cream.

1 Preheat the oven to 400°F/200°C. Grease a large, oval gratin dish, about 10½ inches/26 cm in diameter, liberally with the butter and give it a generous coating of sugar.

2 Spread the apricots evenly cut side up over the bottom of the prepared dish and set aside.

3 In a large bowl, whisk the eggs, cream, and sugar together with the rosemary until light and fluffy, then fold in the flour. Pour the mixture carefully over the apricots, taking care not to dislodge them.

4 Bake in the preheated oven for 25 minutes, or until puffed up and set. Dust with sugar and serve warm or at room temperature.

Serves 6

1 tbsp butter

10½ oz/300 g apricots, halved and pitted

6 eggs, beaten

1 cup heavy cream

¾ cup superfine sugar, plus extra for coating and dusting

1 tsp finely chopped fresh rosemary

scant ⅔ cup all-purpose flour, sifted

Strawberry Shortcake

This recipe is based on the traditional strawberry shortcake with a sconelike base, which was originally adapted from a sweet bread recipe, unlike the rich, buttery, cookie-like shortbread of Scottish origin.

1 Preheat the oven to 400°F/200°C. Lightly grease an 8-inch/20-cm loose-based cake pan.

2 To make the base, sift the flour into a large bowl, then add the butter and rub in with your fingertips until the mixture resembles fine breadcrumbs. Add the superfine sugar. Stir in enough of the milk to form a soft but smooth dough. Gently press the dough evenly into the prepared cake pan. Bake in the preheated oven for 15–20 minutes or until risen, firm to the touch, and golden brown. Let cool for 5 minutes in the pan, then turn out onto a wire rack and let cool completely.

3 To make the topping, beat the milk and mascarpone cheese together with 3 tablespoons of the superfine sugar in a bowl until smooth and fluffy. Put the strawberries in a separate bowl and sprinkle with the remaining superfine sugar and the orange rind.

4 Spread the mascarpone mixture over the scone base and pile the strawberries on top. Spoon over any juices left over from the strawberries in the bowl, then scatter with mint leaves and dust with confectioners' sugar, if desired. Serve immediately.

Serves 6–8

Base

1⅔ cups self-rising flour

scant ½ stick butter, diced, plus extra for greasing

¼ cup superfine sugar

½–⅔ cup milk

Topping

4 tbsp milk

1 lb 2 oz/500 g mascarpone cheese

5 tbsp superfine sugar

1 lb 2 oz/500 g strawberries, hulled and quartered

finely grated rind of 1 orange

To serve

fresh mint leaves

confectioners' sugar, for dusting (optional)

Nectarine Ricotta Mousse with Cinnamon-dusted Wonton Dippers

Serves 4

scant ½ cup heavy cream

3 egg whites

9 oz/250 g ricotta cheese

3 cups superfine sugar

grated rind of ½ orange

3 whole ripe nectarines, pitted and chopped, plus 1 for decoration

Wonton Dippers

6 wonton wrappers

1 tbsp superfine sugar

pinch of ground cinnamon

sunflower oil, for deep-frying

Ricotta gives this mousse a lovely light texture that doesn't require gelatin, but it is best eaten within 2–3 hours of making, if possible.

1 Pour the cream into a large bowl and whip until it forms soft peaks. In a separate bowl, whisk the egg whites until firm and glossy. In a third bowl, beat the ricotta cheese, sugar, and orange rind together until smooth. Fold the cream, orange rind, and nectarines into the ricotta mixture until thoroughly combined. Finally, fold in the egg whites, keeping the mixture loose and fluffy. Spoon into pretty dessert glasses and refrigerate until required.

2 Cut the wonton wrappers into long ribbons just slightly less than ½ inch/1 cm wide. Mix the sugar and cinnamon together. Heat the oil in a deep fat-fryer or wok to 350–375°F/180–190°C, or until a cube of bread browns in 30 seconds. Add the wonton ribbons, in small batches, and cook for 1–2 minutes, or until golden. Remove with a slotted spoon and drain on paper towels. Dust with the cinnamon sugar and let cool on a wire rack.

3 When you are ready to serve, arrange the wonton dippers on a pretty plate and serve alongside the nectarine mousses, decorated with slices of nectarine.

Fall

There are still plenty of fresh vegetables and fruit ready for harvesting in the golden days of fall, such as pumpkins, corn, apples, and blackberries. Nuts, including hazelnuts and walnuts, are also at their best at this time of year. Collect what you can and store as much as possible to provide you with nutritious food as the nights start to draw in.

Crab Fritters
with Avocado Salsa

Crab and corn are perfect together. Add a tangy fruit salsa and the combination tastes every bit as good as it looks!

1 First make the salsa. Put the onion in a bowl. Remove the stalks and seeds from the bell peppers, and cut the flesh into ½-inch/1-cm dice. Add to the onion. Peel the avocado and mango, then remove the pits and cut the flesh into ½-inch/1-cm dice. Add to the bowl. Chop the tomatoes into ½-inch/1-cm dice and add to the other ingredients. Stir in the lime juice and rind and cilantro. Season to taste with salt and pepper.

2 Put the corn kernels, flour, and eggs in a separate bowl and stir until well mixed. Lightly fold in the crabmeat and parsley, and season to taste with salt and pepper.

3 Heat the oil in a large skillet over medium-high heat. Drop spoonfuls of the batter into the hot oil and cook in batches for 2–3 minutes on each side, or until crisp and golden. Remove and drain on paper towels. Serve immediately with the salsa and serve with lime wedges.

Variation
For salsa with a little more bite, add a small finely chopped red chile or a shake or two of Tabasco sauce.

Serves 4

2 cups lightly cooked corn kernels

scant ½ cup all-purpose flour

2 eggs, beaten

10½ oz/300 g cooked white crabmeat

1 small bunch fresh parsley, chopped

3–4 tbsp olive oil

salt and pepper

lime wedges, for serving

Avocado Salsa

1 small red onion, finely chopped

1 red bell pepper

1 yellow bell pepper

1 firm but ripe avocado

1 firm but ripe mango

4 firm but ripe tomatoes

juice and finely grated rind of 2 limes

1 large bunch fresh cilantro, chopped

Bleu Cheese, Fig, and Walnut Bread

Makes 1 loaf

butter, for greasing

3 oz/85 g dried figs, coarsely chopped

4 tbsp Marsala

1⅓ cups all-purpose flour

1 tbsp baking powder

3 eggs

scant 1 cup full-fat crème fraîche

6 oz/175 g bleu cheese, such as Roquefort or Gorgonzola

¾ cup walnuts, coarsely chopped

salt and pepper

A couple of chunky-cut slices of this bread make a great accompaniment to a pear and arugula salad.

1 Lightly grease and line the bottom and sides of a 1-lb/450-g loaf pan with parchment or wax paper. Put the figs in a small bowl, then pour over the Marsala and let soak for 30 minutes or so.

2 Preheat the oven to 350°F/180°C.

3 Sift the flour and baking powder into a large bowl. In a separate bowl, beat the eggs and crème fraîche together until smooth. Stir the egg mixture into the flour until everything is well combined. Season to taste with salt and a good grinding of pepper.

4 Crumble the bleu cheese and add 5½ oz/150 g to the batter. Add the figs and the Marsala, then stir in half the walnuts. Turn the mixture into the prepared pan, then scatter over the remaining cheese and walnuts and bake in the preheated oven for 40 minutes, or until the loaf is golden brown.

5 Cover the pan loosely with foil and return to the oven for an additional 15 minutes, or until a skewer inserted into the center of the loaf comes out clean.

6 Let the loaf cool slightly in the pan, then turn out onto a wire rack to cool completely.

Raspberry and Chile Vinegar

This vinegar is ideal for using in dressings, and also works well with fish and game.

1 Put all the ingredients in a saucepan and heat over low heat, stirring, until the sugar has completely dissolved. Bubble gently for 2–3 minutes to infuse the chile flakes, then remove from the heat. Let the mixture cool.

2 Pour through a sieve lined with butter cheesecloth and store in sterilized bottles.

Cook's Tip
Store the vinegar in a cool, dark place—it should keep for up to a year or so.

Makes 2½ cups

2½ cups white wine vinegar

1–2 tsp chile flakes

½ cup superfine sugar

1 lb 10 oz/750 g raspberries

This is a lovely starter or accompaniment to roast meats.

1 Preheat the oven to 350°F/180°C.

2 Cut horizontally straight through the top quarter of the pumpkin to form a lid. Scoop out the seeds. Put the pumpkin in a large, deep ovenproof dish. Heat the cream and garlic together in a saucepan until just below boiling point. Remove from the heat, then season to taste with salt and pepper and stir in the thyme. Pour into the pumpkin and pop the lid on top.

3 Bake in the preheated oven for 1 hour, or until the flesh is tender—the exact cooking time will depend on the size of the pumpkin. Take care not to overcook the pumpkin, or it may collapse. Remove from the oven, then lift off the lid and scatter over the Gruyère cheese. Return to the oven and bake for an additional 10 minutes.

4 Serve the soft pumpkin flesh with a generous portion of the cheesy cream, some good crusty bread, and a salad of peppery watercress, arugula, or spinach leaves.

Pumpkin and Gruyère Dip

Serves 4

1 large pumpkin

1¼ cups heavy cream

3 garlic cloves, thinly sliced

1 tbsp fresh thyme leaves

4½ oz/125 g grated Gruyère cheese

salt and pepper

For serving

crusty bread

watercress, arugula, or spinach salad

Sea Trout and Ginger Crêpes

This is an unusual main course that works well as a family meal but is equally good for a dinner party.

1 To make the crêpes, put the eggs, milk, and melted butter in a food processor or blender and whiz to combine. Mix the flour and salt together, then add to the egg mixture and whiz again until you have a smooth batter. Let stand for 30 minutes–1 hour or longer, if possible.

2 Lightly grease a nonstick skillet or crêpe pan with some of the butter for pan-frying and heat over medium-high heat until hot. Pour in a small amount of batter (scant ¼ cup, depending on the size of your pan), tilting the pan to spread the mixture over the entire bottom. Cook for 1–2 minutes, or until the crêpe is golden on the underside and little bubbles have started to appear across the surface. Using a palette knife, gently loosen the crêpe around the edges and turn over. Cook for an additional minute, or until golden brown. Repeat until all the remaining batter is used up—it should make eight crêpes.

3 To make the filling, cut the fish into largish chunks. Heat the olive oil in a skillet over medium-high heat, then add the fish and cook, stirring, for 2–3 minutes, or until light golden. Pour over the lemon juice and gently stir in the preserved ginger, currants, and 2 tbsp of the melted butter. Let cool, then fold in the cilantro. Season to taste with salt and pepper.

4 Preheat the oven to 375°F/190°C. Lightly brush an ovenproof dish with melted butter.

5 Lay a crêpe out flat and spoon one-eighth of the mixture onto the center. Fold into a flat parcel. Repeat with the remaining crêpes and arrange alongside the original crêpe, seam-side down, in the prepared dish. Drizzle over the remaining melted butter and cook in the preheated oven for 20–25 minutes, or until the tops of the crêpes are crisp and golden.

6 To make the pesto, put the basil, Parmesan cheese, pine nuts, garlic, and lemon juice into a food processor or blender and whiz to combine. Add enough of the extra virgin olive oil to give a slightly runny but textured consistency. Season with a little sea salt. Cover and refrigerate until ready to use. Serve the crêpes straight from the oven with a drizzle of the pesto.

Serves 4

Crêpes

2 eggs

1¼ cups milk

2 tbsp butter, melted and cooled, plus 2 tbsp for pan-frying and extra (melted) for greasing

scant 1 cup all-purpose flour, sifted

pinch of salt

Filling

1 lb 2 oz/500 g sea trout fillets, skinned and pin-boned

4 tbsp olive oil

juice of ½ lemon

3–4 pieces preserved ginger, chopped

2 tbsp currants

scant ½ stick butter, melted and cooled

1 tbsp chopped fresh cilantro

salt and pepper

Pesto

2 large handfuls fresh basil

½ cup finely grated Parmesan cheese

⅓ cup pine nuts

2 garlic cloves, crushed

juice of ½ lemon

6 tbsp extra virgin olive oil

salt

Roast Duck Breasts with Pear, Ginger, and Onion Marmalade

Serves 4

4 duck breasts, about 6½ oz/ 185 g each

2 tbsp runny honey

salt and pepper

freshly cooked vegetables, for serving

Onion Marmalade

scant ½ stick butter

2 ripe but firm pears, peeled, cored and sliced

6 onions, sliced

2 tbsp dark chestnut honey

2 pieces preserved ginger

2 tbsp preserved ginger syrup

Roast duck breasts are so easy to prepare. Add a lovely sticky-sweet marmalade made from ripe fall pears, slow-cooked with onions and preserved ginger, and the results are fantastic.

1 Preheat the oven to 400°F/200°C.

2 To make the marmalade, melt the butter in a saucepan over medium-high heat, then add the pears and onions and cook, stirring occasionally, for 10 minutes, or until soft and golden. Add the honey, preserved ginger, and ginger syrup and bubble gently for 15–20 minutes, or until the mixture is sticky and caramelized. Season to taste with salt and pepper. Keep warm until ready to serve, if necessary.

3 Meanwhile, heat a skillet over medium-high heat until hot. Add the duck breasts, skin-side down, to the hot skillet. There is no need to add any fat; the breasts will release plenty as they cook. Cook for 2–3 minutes, or until golden brown. Turn the breasts over and cook for an additional 2–3 minutes. Transfer the breasts to a roasting dish, then brush with the honey and season to taste with salt and pepper. Roast in the preheated oven for 12 minutes. Remove from the oven and let rest in a warm place for 5 minutes.

4 To serve, cut each duck breast into slices and fan out on each of four warmed dinner plates. Serve immediately with the onion marmalade and freshly cooked vegetables.

Chicken and Fall Vegetable Casserole

You could ring the changes by using any fall vegetable that looks good on shopping day, but this mix works especially well.

1 Preheat the oven to 350°F/180°C.

2 Heat the oil in a large skillet over medium heat, then add the leeks and garlic and cook, stirring frequently, for 3–4 minutes, or until softened. Add the chicken and cook, stirring frequently, for 5 minutes. Add the sweet potatoes and parsnips and cook, stirring frequently, for 5 minutes, or until golden and beginning to soften. Add the bell peppers and mushrooms and cook, stirring frequently, for 5 minutes. Stir in the tomatoes, rice, and parsley and season to taste with salt and pepper.

3 Spoon the mixture into an ovenproof dish. Scatter over the cheddar cheese and bake in the preheated oven for 20–25 minutes. Serve immediately with a salad, if desired.

Variation
You can substitute squash, such as butternut, for the sweet potatoes.

Serves 4

3 tbsp olive oil

2 leeks, sliced

2 garlic cloves, sliced

2 large chicken breasts, about 6 oz/175 g each, cut into bite-size pieces

2 sweet potatoes, peeled and cut into chunks

2 parsnips, scrubbed and sliced

1 red bell pepper, seeded and cut into strips

1 yellow bell pepper, seeded and cut into strips

9 oz/250 g mixed wild mushrooms, cleaned

14 oz/400 g tomatoes, coarsely chopped

4 cups cooked white long-grain rice

1 small bunch fresh parsley, chopped

generous 1 cup grated sharp cheddar cheese

salt and pepper

salad, for serving (optional)

Carrot Tart Tatin

Crisp, golden pastry and sweet young carrots make a wonderful combination.

1 Preheat the oven to 400°F/200°C.

2 Cook the carrots in a saucepan of boiling water for 10–15 minutes, or until just tender. Drain, then toss with the honey, butter, and thyme and season to taste with salt and pepper. Spoon over the base of an 8-inch/20-cm tart tatin pan or round cake pan with a depth of about 1¼ inches/3 cm and roast in the preheated oven for 15 minutes, or until the carrots are caramelized.

3 Roll the pastry out on a floured work surface into a round large enough to fit the pan and give a ¾-inch/ 2-cm overlap. Lay the pastry carefully over the carrots and tuck the edges down between the carrots and the side of the tin to make a border. Bake in the oven for 15 minutes, or until the pastry is puffed and golden.

4 Remove the tart from the oven and turn the pan over onto a plate to release. Serve immediately.

Serves 4

1 lb 5 oz/600 g young carrots, peeled and cut into 1-inch/ 2.5-cm chunks

2 tbsp runny honey

scant ½ stick butter

1 small bunch fresh thyme, chopped

12 oz/350 g puff pastry, thawed if frozen

all-purpose flour, for dusting

salt and pepper

Roast Pork with Rosemary Potatoes

A classic pairing and one that is hard to beat.

1 Preheat the oven to 425°F/220°C.

2 Make sure that the skin of the pork is well scored and dry. Put into a roasting pan. Brush the skin with 1 tablespoon of the oil and liberally rub with salt. Roast in the preheated oven for 20 minutes, or until the skin has started to blister and crisp. Reduce the heat to 400°F/200°C and roast for an additional 40 minutes, or until the pork is cooked through and the skin is crisp and golden. Remove from the oven and ensure that the juices run clear when a skewer is inserted deep into the meat. Let it rest for 20 minutes before slicing.

3 Meanwhile, for the rosemary potatoes, peel the potatoes and cut into medium dice. Heat the oil in a separate roasting pan in the oven. When hot, add the potatoes and rosemary, then toss to coat and roast for 40 minutes, or until crisp and golden. Remove from the pan and scatter with a little salt. Serve immediately with the sliced pork.

Serves 4

1 leg of pork, weighing 2 lb 4 oz/1 kg

3 tbsp olive oil

salt

Rosemary Potatoes

2 lb 4 oz/1 kg starchy potatoes

4 tbsp olive oil

1 bunch fresh rosemary, chopped

Venison Steaks with Fig and Walnut Relish

Venison is low in calories and fat, and makes the perfect fast food.

1 To make the relish, chop the figs and mix with the walnuts in a bowl. Stir in the garlic, walnut oil and balsamic vinegar. Season to taste with salt and pepper and set aside.

2 Mix 2 tablespoons of the olive oil and the rosemary together and rub over the venison steaks. Cover and let marinate in a cool place for 30 minutes, if possible.

3 Heat the remaining oil in a skillet over medium-high heat. Season the steaks to taste with salt and pepper, then add to the skillet and cook for 2–3 minutes on each side, or until cooked to your liking. Venison is very lean meat and can easily become tough if overcooked. Remove and keep warm. Deglaze the skillet with the wine, stirring in any sticky bits from the bottom of the pan. Bubble for 2–3 minutes, then add the butter and stir until smooth and glossy.

4 To serve, top the steaks with a spoonful of the relish and drizzle with the sauce.

Serves 4

3 tbsp olive oil

2 fresh sprigs of rosemary, finely chopped

4 venison steaks, about 6 oz/ 175 g each

scant ½ cup red wine

2 tbsp butter

salt and pepper

Walnut Relish

4 ripe figs

3 tbsp walnuts, toasted and chopped

1 garlic clove, crushed

1 tbsp walnut oil

1–2 tsp balsamic vinegar

Crispy Parmesan-coated Sea Bass

Serves 4

4 sea bass fillets, about 4½ oz/ 125 g each, skin on and pin boned

3 tbsp olive oil

juice and grated rind of 1 lemon

1 cup finely grated Parmesan cheese

1 small bunch fresh parsley, finely chopped

salt and pepper

For serving

watercress, arugula, or spinach salad

lemon wedges

Parmesan cheese, parsley, and lemon make a really top-notch trio to top broiled sea bass, adding a delicious flavor without overpowering the delicate fish.

1 Preheat the broiler to its highest setting. Brush the broiler pan with a little of the oil and lay the fillets in the broiler pan, skin-down. Drizzle over a little of the remaining oil, then give each fillet a good squeeze of lemon juice and season with salt and pepper.

2 Mix the lemon rind, Parmesan cheese, and parsley together and scatter evenly over the fish. Drizzle over the remaining oil. Cook under the broiler for 4 minutes, or until the fish is just cooked and golden—the exact cooking time will depend on the thickness of the fillets. Serve immediately with a salad of watercress, arugula, or spinach leaves and lemon wedges.

Serves 4

10½ oz/300 g ripe but firm plums

3 tbsp superfine sugar, or to taste, plus extra for dusting

scant ¼ cup water

1 tsp vanilla extract

8 x 8-inch/20-cm squares filo dough

scant ½ stick butter, melted

3 tbsp stale cake crumbs

sour cream or ice cream, for serving

Little Vanilla Plum Strudels

These pretty, crisp little strudels filled with sweet, vanilla-scented plums, are so impressive yet amazingly quick and easy to make.

1 Preheat the oven to 400°F/200°C.

2 Halve the plums and remove the pits. Dice the flesh and put in a saucepan with the sugar and water. Cook over gentle heat for 15 minutes, or until soft. Stir in the vanilla extract and let cool.

3 Lay out 4 squares of filo dough and brush with some of the melted butter. Top each with the remaining dough squares. Scatter an equal quantity of the cake crumbs down the center and spoon one-quarter of the plum mixture on top of each. Brush the dough edges with a little more melted butter, then fold them in and roll up to form four individual strudels. Lay, seam-side down, on a baking sheet, then brush with melted butter and bake in the preheated oven for 6–8 minutes, or until golden.

4 Remove from the oven, then brush again with the remaining melted butter and dust with sugar. Serve with sour cream or ice cream.

Variation

You could use stale white breadcrumbs instead of the cake crumbs.

Pears are another seasonal treat not to be missed. For the best results when cooking, choose fragrant pears that are free of blemishes and still quite firm.

1 Preheat the oven to 300°F/150°C.

2 Peel the pears, then remove the central cores and cut into quarters. Rub with the lemon juice and sit in an ovenproof dish. Scatter over the sugar, then pour over the wine and add the cinnamon stick. Cover with a lid or foil and bake in the preheated oven for 1¼ hours, or until the pears are soft and the liquid is syrupy, stirring halfway through.

3 To make the sauce, put the cream, sugar, and cardamom seeds in a saucepan and heat over gentle heat for 2–3 minutes to infuse. Mix the milk and cornstarch together until smooth, then stir into the cream mixture. Increase the heat slightly and cook, stirring constantly, until slightly thickened. Pour the mixture through a fine sieve to remove the seeds and serve with the warm pears.

Slow-baked Pears with Cardamom Cream Sauce

Serves 4

4 pears

juice of ½ lemon

½ cup solidly packed brown sugar

1¼ cups red wine

1 cinnamon stick

Cardamom Cream Sauce

2 cups heavy cream

¼ cup superfine sugar

seeds from 6 cardamom pods

3 tbsp milk

1 tsp cornstarch

Butternut Squash and Cinnamon Tart

Serves 6–8

Pastry

1½ sticks salted butter, softened

¼ cup superfine sugar

1 egg yolk

scant 2 cups all-purpose flour, sifted, plus extra for dusting

Filling

14 oz/400 g peeled and deseeded butternut squash

¾ cup soft light solidly packed brown sugar

3 eggs, beaten

1 tsp ground cinnamon

3 tbsp dark rum

2 tbsp mascarpone cheese

vanilla ice cream or cream, for serving

Butternut squash makes an unusual but surprisingly delicious filling for a sweet tart.

1 To make the pastry, beat the butter and sugar together in a bowl until light and fluffy. Add the egg yolk and stir until fully incorporated and smooth. Gradually add the flour and mix until the dough forms a ball, taking care not to overwork. Divide in half and freeze one half. Wrap the remaining pastry in plastic wrap and let rest at room temperature for 20 minutes or so.

2 Roll the pastry out on a floured work surface and use to line a 9-inch/23-cm tart pan with a removable base. Refrigerate until required.

3 Preheat the oven to 350°F/180°C.

4 To make the filling, cut the squash into small chunks and cook in a saucepan of boiling water until tender. Drain and transfer to a food processor or blender, then whiz to a purée. Add the remaining filling ingredients and whiz again until smooth. Set the tart pan on a baking sheet and carefully fill to three-quarters full with the mixture. Transfer to the preheated oven and bake for 10–15 minutes, or until the filling is beginning to set. Pour in the remaining mixture and bake for an additional 25 minutes, or until set.

5 Remove from the oven and let cool. Serve in slices with vanilla ice cream or cream.

Cook's Tip

The pastry recipe yields enough for two tarts, but contains one egg yolk and so is impractical to make less. Simply freeze half and you have pastry ready for next time.

Blackberry Soup with Buttermilk Custards

Sweet and inky blackberry soup and wobbly buttermilk custards make the most sublime combination.

1 To make the custards, put the gelatin in a small bowl, then cover with cold water and let soak for 5 minutes. Meanwhile, heat the buttermilk, cream, and milk together in a saucepan to just below boiling point. Add the sugar and stir until it has completely dissolved. Remove the gelatin from the soaking liquid and squeeze out any excess water. Add to the hot buttermilk mixture and stir until completely dissolved. Pour through a fine sieve and fill four dariole molds or individual ovenproof molds. Transfer to the refrigerator and chill for several hours, or overnight, until set.

2 To make the soup, put the blackberries, wine, and water in a large saucepan with the sugar and star anise. Simmer very gently for 8–10 minutes, or until the sugar has dissolved and the mixture has a lovely anise scent. Remove from the heat and let cool. Once the mixture has cooled, remove the star anise, then transfer the mixture to a food processor and whiz until smooth. Alternatively, use a hand-held blender to whiz the soup until smooth in the saucepan. Pour through a fine sieve and stir in the Mûre, if using. Cover and refrigerate until ready to serve.

3 To serve, divide the soup between four soup plates (rather than deep bowls) and set a buttermilk custard in the center of each.

Serves 4

Buttermilk Custards

4 sheets leaf gelatin

generous 1 cup buttermilk

generous 1 cup heavy cream

¼ cup milk

½ cup superfine sugar

Blackberry Soup

1 lb/450 g blackberries

1¼ cups fruity red wine

scant ½ cup water

⅓ cup superfine sugar, or to taste

2 star anise

4–5 tbsp Mûre liqueur (optional)

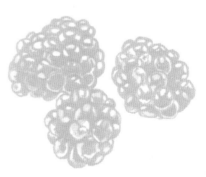

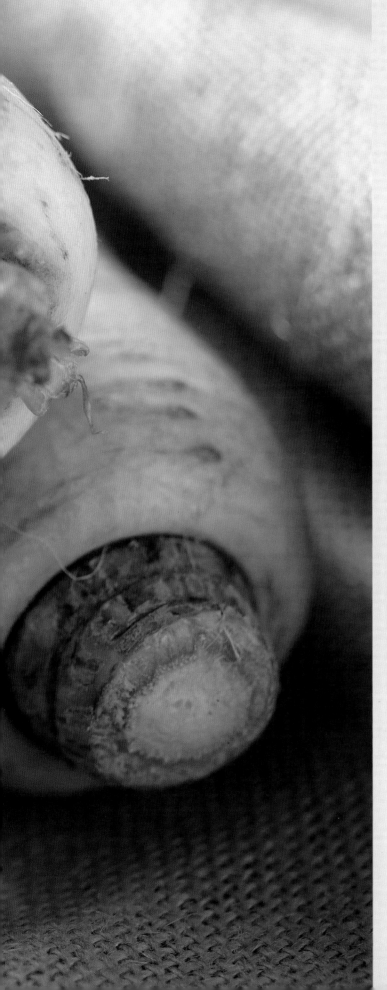

Winter

Although the winter can seem a little bleak, making comfort food for sharing with family and friends is the perfect antidote. This doesn't necessarily mean that you have to spend longer in the kitchen—warming casseroles, braises, soups, and stews can all bubble away happily while you get on with other tasks. And there's all the excitement of the delicious treats and luxurious food that comes with the festive season!

Grilled Scallops with Crispy Leeks

Look for plump, diver-caught scallops where possible and avoid ones that have been pre-frozen—they will merely thaw into something totally bland, with the taste and texture of damp cotton wool.

1 Trim the leeks and roughly chop five of them. Halve the remaining leek, then cut into very fine julienne and reserve. Heat the butter in a skillet over medium heat, then add the chopped leeks and cook, stirring frequently, for 5 minutes, or until softened but not colored. Add the honey, then season to taste with salt and pepper and keep warm.

2 Meanwhile, heat the oil for deep-frying in a deep-fat fryer or wok to 350–375°F/180–190°C, or until a cube of bread browns in 30 seconds. Add the leek julienne to the hot oil and cook until crisp and golden. Remove with a slotted spoon and drain on paper towels. Lightly scatter with sea salt flakes.

3 Heat a ridged grill pan over high heat. Brush the scallops with the olive oil, then add to the hot grill pan and cook for a little over 1 minute on each side. Remove from the heat and season with lemon juice to taste and a light sprinkling of salt.

4 Place a dollop of buttered leeks onto each of six warmed serving plates. Top each with 3 scallops, then add a tangle of crispy leeks and serve immediately.

Serves 6

6 chunky leeks

scant ½ stick butter

1 scant tsp thick-set honey

olive or sunflower oil, for deep-frying

18 plump raw scallops, shelled and cleaned

1–2 tbsp olive oil

freshly squeezed lemon juice, to taste

salt and pepper

sea salt flakes

Celeriac Soup with Cheese Pastry Sticks

Serves 4

3 tbsp olive oil

1 onion, chopped

1 celeriac, peeled and cut into chunks

4 cups good-quality vegetable stock

1 small bunch fresh thyme, chopped; reserving whole sprigs, for garnish

salt and pepper

Cheese Pastry Sticks

butter, for greasing

13 oz/375 g puff pastry, thawed if frozen

all-purpose flour, for dusting

1 egg, beaten

1 cup finely grated Parmesan cheese

Gnarled and knobbly celeriac wouldn't win any prizes for appearance, but it does have a fabulous celery-like flavor and makes great soups and gratins.

1 Heat the oil in a large saucepan over medium heat, then add the onion and cook, stirring frequently, for 4–5 minutes, or until softened but not colored. Add the celeriac and cook, stirring frequently, for 3–4 minutes. Pour in the stock and add the thyme. Simmer for 25 minutes, or until the celeriac is tender.

2 Meanwhile, preheat the oven to 400°F/200°C. Lightly grease two baking sheets.

3 For the pastry sticks, roll the pastry out thinly on a floured work surface. Brush with half the egg and scatter over half the Parmesan cheese. Add a good grinding of pepper. Fold the pastry in half. Brush with the remaining egg, then scatter with the remaining cheese and add another grinding of pepper. Cut into strips about ½ inch/1 cm wide. Twist the pastry strips gently along their length to produce spiral shapes. Bake in the preheated oven for 5 minutes, or until crisp and golden.

4 Transfer the soup to a food processor and whiz until smooth. Alternatively, use a hand-hand blender to whiz the soup until smooth in the saucepan. Gently reheat the soup in the saucepan. Season to taste with salt and pepper.

5 Pour the soup into warmed bowls, and garnish with thyme sprigs. Serve alongside the warm pastry sticks.

Sweet Potato Ravioli with Sage Butter

Serves 4

Pasta

14 oz/400 g type 00 pasta flour

4 eggs, beaten

semolina, for dusting

salt

Filling

1 lb 2 oz/500 g sweet potatoes

3 tbsp olive oil

1 large onion, finely chopped

1 garlic clove, crushed

1 tsp fresh thyme leaves, chopped

2 tbsp runny honey

salt and pepper

Sage Butter

scant ½ stick butter

1 bunch fresh sage leaves finely chopped, reserving a few leaves for garnish

Making homemade ravioli does take a little time, but it is very therapeutic and the end results are highly rewarding.

1 To make the pasta, sift the flour into a large bowl or food processor. Add the eggs and bring the mixture together or process to make a soft but not sticky dough. Turn out onto a work surface lightly dusted with semolina and knead for 4–5 minutes, or until smooth. Cover with plastic wrap and refrigerate for at least 30 minutes.

2 For the filling, peel the sweet potatoes and cut into chunks. Cook in a saucepan of boiling water for 20 minutes, or until tender. Drain and mash.

3 Heat the oil in a skillet over medium heat, then add the onion and cook, stirring frequently, for 4–5 minutes, or until softened but not colored. Stir the onion into the mashed potatoes and add the garlic and thyme leaves. Drizzle with the honey and season to taste with salt and pepper. Set aside.

4 Using a pasta machine, roll the pasta out to a thickness of about $\frac{1}{32}$ inch/1 mm (or use a rolling pin on a work surface lightly dusted with semolina, and plenty of elbow grease). Cut the pasta in half. Place teaspoonfuls of the filling at evenly spaced intervals across one half of the pasta. Brush around the filling with a small amount of water and cover with the second half. Press lightly around the filling to seal the pasta and cut into squares with a sharp knife or pastry wheel. Lay the ravioli out on a sheet of wax paper that has been lightly dusted with semolina.

5 Bring a large saucepan of salted water to a boil and drop in the ravioli. Cook for 2–3 minutes until the pasta rises to the surface and is tender but still retaining a little bite.

6 Meanwhile, for the sage butter, melt the butter with the sage in a small saucepan over gentle heat.

7 Drain the ravioli and immediately toss with the sage butter. Serve immediately, garnished with sage leaves.

Easy Duck Rillettes with Homemade Fennel Bread Toast

Serves 4

4–6 duck legs

1 bunch fresh thyme

salt and pepper

Fennel Bread

1 lb 2 oz/500 g white bread flour, plus extra for dusting

¼ oz/7 g active dry yeast

1 tsp salt

1 tbsp extra virgin olive oil, plus extra for oiling

1 tbsp whole grain mustard

3 tbsp fennel seeds

generous ¾ cup warm water

Slow-cooked duck and homemade fennel-flecked bread make a great starter or light lunch.

1 Preheat the oven to 275°F/140°C.

2 Lay the duck legs in a roasting pan and season to taste with salt and pepper. Scatter over the thyme. Roast in the preheated oven for 2½ hours. Pour the rendered fat into a small bowl and reserve. Remove any skin from the legs and strip the meat from the bones. Using two forks, pull the meat into shreds. Scrape the meaty deposits from the bottom of the pan, then stir into the shredded meat and divide between four ramekins. Push the meat down and add just enough of the reserved rendered fat to cover. Refrigerate until ready to use, but remove 30 minutes before serving.

3 To make the bread, put the flour in a bowl and stir in the yeast. Add the salt and mix well. Stir in the oil, mustard, fennel seeds, and enough of the water to bring the dough together into a soft but not sticky dough. Turn the dough out onto a floured work surface and knead for 5–10 minutes, or until smooth and elastic. Form into a loaf shape and lay on an oiled baking sheet. Let rise in a warm place for 40 minutes, or until doubled in size.

4 Preheat the oven to 425°F/220°C.

5 Bake the bread in the preheated oven for 20 minutes, or until the loaf is golden and crisp on top and makes a hollow sound when tapped on the base. Remove from the oven and let cool on a wire rack.

6 Just before serving, slice the bread thinly, then toast until golden and serve alongside the rillettes.

Serves 4

3 tbsp olive oil

1 lb 5 oz/600 g parsnips, peeled and thinly sliced

1 tsp fresh thyme leaves

1 tsp superfine sugar

1¼ cups heavy cream

1 lb 5 oz/600 g tomatoes, thinly sliced

1 tsp dried oregano

1½ cups grated cheddar cheese

salt and pepper

Parsnip and Tomato Casserole

Serve with salad and fresh crusty bread as a delicious vegetarian supper, or as a side dish with roast or grilled meat or chops.

1 Preheat the oven to 350°F/180°C.

2 Heat the oil in a skillet over medium heat, then add the parsnips, thyme, sugar, and salt and pepper to taste and cook, stirring frequently, for 6–8 minutes, or until golden and softened.

3 Spread half the parsnips over the bottom of a gratin dish. Pour over half the cream, then arrange half the tomatoes in an even layer across the parsnips. Season to taste with salt and pepper and scatter over half the oregano. Sprinkle over half the cheddar cheese. Top with the remaining parsnips and tomatoes. Sprinkle with the remaining oregano, then season to taste with salt and pepper and pour over the remaining cream. Scatter over the remaining cheese.

4 Cover with foil and bake in the preheated oven for 40 minutes, or until the parsnips are tender. Remove the foil and return to the oven for an additional 5–10 minutes, or until the top is golden and bubbling. Serve immediately.

Potato, Cheese, and Bacon Gratin

Serves 4

2 lb 4 oz/1 kg small waxy potatoes, sliced

2 tbsp olive oil

3 garlic cloves, peeled but kept whole

5½ oz/150 g bacon lardons

2 tbsp fresh thyme leaves

2½ cups heavy cream

7 oz/200 g Reblochon cheese or any other good melting cheese, sliced

salt and pepper

A favorite après-ski dish, and a winning one-dish supper for winter nights.

1 Preheat the oven to 350°F/180°C.

2 Cook the potato slices in a large saucepan of boiling water for 10–15 minutes, or until just tender. Drain.

3 Heat the oil in a large skillet over medium heat. Hit the garlic cloves with the back of a sturdy knife to split them and add to the skillet. Add the bacon lardons and cook for 3–4 minutes, or until just cooked. Add the potato slices and cook for 3–4 minutes. Pour in the cream, then add the thyme leaves and stir well.

4 Transfer the mixture to a gratin dish and top with the cheese slices. Bake in the preheated oven for 20 minutes, or until golden and bubbling.

Cook's Tip

This is especially delicious served with peppery salad greens and good crusty bread.

Spinach and Ricotta Rollatini

This is a delicious dish that makes a great one-dish bake in much the way that lasagne does. It takes time to prepare, but the results are well worth the effort.

1 To make the pasta, sift the flour and a pinch of salt together into a large bowl or food processor. Add the eggs and bring the mixture together or process to make a soft but not sticky dough. Turn out onto a work surface lightly dusted with semolina and knead for 4–5 minutes, or until smooth. Cover with plastic wrap and refrigerate for at least 30 minutes.

2 For the filling, heat the oil in a skillet over medium heat, then add the garlic and onion and cook, stirring frequently, for 3–4 minutes, or until softened but not colored. Quarter the tomatoes, then remove the cores and seeds and coarsely chop the flesh. Add to the skillet and cook for 5 minutes, or until sticky and soft. Remove from the heat and let cool.

3 Meanwhile, put the spinach in a large saucepan with only the water that is left clinging to the leaves after washing and cook over medium heat for 2–3 minutes, or until just wilted. Drain and let cool. Squeeze out any excess moisture and chop. Stir into the tomatoes. Add the ricotta cheese and stir until everything is thoroughly combined. Season to taste with salt and pepper.

4 Roll the pasta out on a work surface lightly dusted with semolina into a rectangular sheet approximately 8 x 10 inch/20 x 25 cm, with a thickness of about 1/16 inch/2 mm. Spread the spinach filling evenly over the pasta, leaving a 1-inch/2.5-cm border around the edges. Carefully roll the dough up to resemble a jelly roll. Wrap in a piece of butter cheesecloth or a clean cloth, tying the ends with clean kitchen string. Fill a long, flameproof roasting pan with salted water and bring to a boil on the stove. Add the pasta roll and simmer for 20 minutes. Remove from the water and let stand for 5 minutes, or until cool enough to handle, but not too cold to eat.

5 Meanwhile, preheat the broiler to high and lightly grease a flameproof gratin dish. Carefully remove the cloth, then cut the pasta roll into slices 5/8 inch/1.5 cm thick. Arrange in the prepared dish, overlapping slightly. Drizzle with the butter and scatter over the Parmesan cheese. Cook under the preheated broiler for 4–5 minutes, or until golden. Serve immediately.

Serves 4

Pasta

2 cups type 00 pasta flour

3 eggs, beaten

semolina, for dusting

salt

Filling

2 tbsp olive oil

1 garlic clove, crushed

1 large onion, finely chopped

1 lb 2 oz/500 g ripe tomatoes

14 oz/400 g young spinach leaves

9 oz/250 g ricotta cheese

salt and pepper

Topping

2 tbsp butter, melted, plus extra for greasing

¼ cup finely grated Parmesan cheese

Roast Goose with Cinnamon-spiced Red Cabbage

Stuffing rich birds such as goose with a heavy stuffing tends to absorb some of the fat and give a greasy result. Much better to go for a crisp golden skin and serve it with cinnamon-spiced red cabbage.

1 Preheat the oven to 400°F/200°C.

2 Cut away any excess fat from the tail area of the goose. Season the goose cavity to taste with salt and pepper and push in the onion quarters, bay leaves, and thyme, reserving a few sprigs for the garnish. Put the goose on a rack set over a roasting pan and prick the skin all over with a skewer. Season the outside of the goose to taste with salt and pepper. Roast in the preheated oven for 15 minutes per 1 lb/450 g, plus an extra 15 minutes. Remove from the oven, then cover loosely with foil and let rest for 15 minutes before carving.

3 While the goose is roasting, prepare the red cabbage. Heat the oil in a large skillet over medium heat, then add the onion and cook, stirring frequently, for 3–4 minutes, or until softened but not colored. Add all the remaining ingredients, then cover and cook for 30–40 minutes, or until the cabbage is tender and the liquid has reduced. Remove the cinnamon stick before serving.

4 Carve the goose and serve in slices, alongside the red cabbage and garnished with the reserved thyme.

Cook's Tip
Crunchy roast potatoes make a great accompaniment to this dish.

Serves 6

1 oven-ready goose, weighing about 10 lb/4.5 kg

2 onions, quartered

1 bunch fresh thyme

2 bay leaves

salt and pepper

Red Cabbage

3 tbsp olive oil

1 large onion, sliced

1 red cabbage, shredded

1 large cooking apple, peeled, cored, and chopped

3 tbsp raisins

1 ¼ cups red wine

scant ¼ cup red wine vinegar

2 tsp superfine sugar, or to taste

1 cinnamon stick

Slow-cooked Lamb with Celeriac

This recipe creates lamb that is well done but still moist. If you prefer pinker lamb, increase the oven temperature and cut down the cooking time.

1 Score gently through the thin coating of fat on the lamb in a diamond pattern, taking care not to pierce the meat. Put in a non-metallic dish. Separate the heads of garlic and remove the papery bits. Peel and crush four of the garlic cloves and reserve the remainder. Mix the crushed garlic, lemon rind and juice, and rosemary together. Add a couple of good pinches of sea salt flakes, and a generous grinding of pepper, then stir in the oil. Rub the mixture all over the meat. Cover and let marinate in the refrigerator for several hours, preferably overnight.

2 Preheat the oven to 425°F/220°C.

3 Transfer the lamb to a roasting pan and pour over any marinade remaining in the dish. Roast in the preheated oven for 20 minutes. Reduce the oven temperature to 375°F/190°C. Add the reserved whole garlic cloves, shallots, and wine to the roasting pan, then cover with foil and roast for an additional 1 hour 40 minutes, basting occasionally. Remove the foil, then add the celeriac chunks and turn to coat in the pan juices. Cook with the lamb for an additional 20 minutes.

4 Remove the roasting pan from the oven, then lift the lamb out and keep warm. Return the roasting pan with the celeriac and garlic to the oven, then turn over in the juices again and roast for an additional 10–15 minutes, or until golden and sticky.

5 Carve the lamb and serve with the celeriac, drizzling over the pan juices. Encourage your guests to squeeze the soft garlic paste from the cloves and smear it over mouthfuls of the lamb as they eat.

Serves 4–6

1 leg of lamb, on the bone, weighing 5 lb 8 oz/2.5 kg

2 whole heads garlic

grated rind of 2 lemons and juice of 1

2 tbsp finely chopped fresh rosemary

3 tbsp extra virgin olive oil

3 shallots, coarsely chopped

1½ cups dry white wine

2 lb 4 oz/1 kg celeriac, peeled and cut into large chunks

sea salt flakes

salt and pepper

Marsala-braised Pork Meatballs with Roast Winter Vegetables

Serves 4

1 lb/450 g fresh ground pork

1 cup finely grated Parmesan cheese

1 tsp dried oregano

2 tsp finely chopped fresh sage

5 onions, sliced

1¼ cups Marsala

2 tbsp runny honey

salt and pepper

Roast Vegetables

4 carrots, peeled and cut into chunks

4 parsnips, scrubbed and cut into chunks

2 sweet potatoes, peeled and cut into chunks

3 leeks, chopped

4 tbsp olive oil

1 small bunch fresh thyme

As an alternative, you could use the same pork mixture to make meat loaf, using a small loaf pan instead.

1 Preheat the oven to 375°F/190°C.

2 For the roast vegetables, toss all the prepared vegetables with 3 tablespoons of the oil and the thyme in a roasting pan. Spread out and roast in the preheated oven for 45 minutes, or until soft and caramelized.

3 Meanwhile, put the pork, Parmesan cheese, oregano, sage, and salt and pepper to taste in a large bowl and mix well. Form into balls about the size of walnuts. Heat the remaining oil in a skillet over medium heat, then add the meatballs and cook for 3–4 minutes, or until golden. Remove with a slotted spoon and transfer to an ovenproof dish.

4 Add the onions to the skillet and cook, stirring frequently, for 5 minutes, or until beginning to color. Add the Marsala and honey and cook for an additional 5 minutes, or until slightly syrupy and glossy. Pour over the meatballs, then transfer to the oven and cook for an additional 20 minutes. Serve immediately with the roast vegetables.

Cook's Tip
Mustardy mashed potatoes make an ideal side dish.

Walnut and Pecorino Scones

These are delicious served at the end of a meal with cheese or sweet preserves.

1 Preheat the oven to 400°F/200°C.

2 Sift the flour and salt into a large bowl. Add the butter and rub in with your fingertips until the mixture resembles fine breadcrumbs. Stir in the sugar, Pecorino cheese, and walnuts. Add enough of the milk to bring the mixture together into a soft but not sticky dough.

3 Gently roll the dough out on a lightly floured work surface to a thickness of 1–1¼ inches/2.5–3 cm. Use a 2½-inch/6-cm round cookie cutter to cut into rounds (make the scones smaller or larger if you prefer).

4 Put the rounds on a baking sheet and bake in the preheated oven for 15 minutes, or until golden and firm. Remove from the oven and let cool on a wire rack.

Cook's Tip
These are also great served alongside vegetable soup, especially a root vegetable one such as parsnip or carrot.

Makes about 10 scones

1 lb/450 g self-rising flour, plus extra for dusting

pinch of salt

¾ stick butter, diced

¼ cup superfine sugar

1¾ oz/50 g Pecorino cheese

1 cup walnut pieces

about 1¼ cups milk

Fresh Orange Salad with Pistachios

Fresh and simple, but nonetheless delicious, this makes a healthy, quick-to-prepare ending to a meal, and works especially well after rich main courses.

1 Put the superfine sugar and water in a heavy-bottom saucepan over low heat and heat until the sugar has completely dissolved.

2 Increase the heat and bubble until the mixture develops a golden caramel color. Remove from the heat and stir in the liqueur, if using. Let cool.

3 Using a zester, remove the zest from two of the oranges in long shreds. Peel all the oranges, taking care to remove all the bitter white pith. Cut the flesh into thin slices, then remove the seeds and arrange on a pretty serving platter. Pour over the cooled caramel syrup. Lightly chop the pistachios and scatter over the oranges.

4 Serve with thick Greek-style yogurt or sour cream.

Serves 4

¼ cup superfine sugar

scant ¼ cup water

2 tbsp orange-flavored liqueur (optional)

6 large juicy oranges

generous ¾ cup pistachios

generous ¾ cup thick Greek-style yogurt or sour cream, for serving

Coffee and Candied Chestnut Cake

Serves 8–10

1½ sticks butter, softened, plus extra for greasing

1 cup dark brown solidly packed sugar

3 eggs, beaten

scant 1¼ cups self-rising flour

1 small measure strong espresso coffee

½ cup candied chestnuts, chopped

Filling and Topping

generous ¾ cup heavy cream

1 tbsp superfine sugar

2 tbsp dark rum

7 squares dark chocolate, melted

This is a decadent cake with a fantastic flavor, packed with chocolate and heaps of rum-flavored cream—definitely not for diet days!

1 Preheat the oven to 325°F/160°C. Lightly grease two 8-inch/20-cm sandwich cake pans.

2 Beat the butter and brown sugar together in a bowl until light and fluffy. Add the eggs, a little at a time, beating after each addition, until they have all been incorporated. Add the flour and coffee and beat until smooth. Fold in the chestnuts. Divide the mixture evenly between the prepared pans.

3 Bake in the preheated oven for 20–25 minutes, or until the cakes have risen and spring back when touched gently with the tip of a index finger. Remove from the oven and let cool for 10 minutes or so in the pans, then turn out onto a wire rack and let cool completely.

4 For the filling and topping, whip the cream, superfine sugar, and rum together in a bowl until thick. Spread half the melted chocolate over one of the cakes. Cover with the cream mixture and place the other cake on top. Spread the remaining melted chocolate over the top of the cake. Serve in slices.

Sticky Apple Cakes with Hazelnut Praline Ice cream

Serves 6

1¼ sticks butter, plus extra for greasing

generous ½ cup dark brown solidly packed sugar

2 eggs, beaten

scant 1 cup self-rising flour

½ tsp baking soda

2 cooking apples, cored and diced

6 tbsp maple syrup

Hazelnut Praline Ice Cream

1⅓ cups superfine sugar

scant ¼ cup water

⅔ cup hazelnuts

1¼ cups milk

6 egg yolks

1¼ cups heavy cream

Use genuine Canadian maple syrup and not the cheap, sugary, artificially flavored substitutes.

1 For the ice cream, put ½ cup of the superfine sugar and water in a heavy-bottom saucepan over low heat and heat until the sugar has dissolved.

2 Increase the heat and bubble the mixture until it develops a dark amber color. Stir in the hazelnuts. Turn the mixture immediately onto a greased baking sheet. Leave until completely cold, then break into very small pieces.

3 Pour the milk into a saucepan and heat to boiling point. Beat the eggs and the remaining superfine sugar together in a heatproof bowl until smooth. Pour the hot milk over the eggs and whisk until smooth. Return the mixture to the saucepan and stir over very low heat until it has thickened enough to coat the back of a spoon. Remove from the heat, then stir in the cream and let cool. Transfer to an ice cream machine and churn according to the manufacturer's directions until almost frozen. Add the hazelnut praline and churn until completely frozen. Freeze until ready to serve. Alternatively, pour the mixture into a freezerproof container and freeze until almost solid. Remove from the freezer and beat until smooth to prevent the formation of ice crystals. Stir in the hazelnut praline. Return to the freezer and freeze until solid. Remove from the freezer 10–15 minutes before serving, to soften a little.

4 Preheat the oven to 350°F/180°C. Lightly grease a baking sheet and 6 ramekins or ⅔-cup ovenproof basins.

5 Beat the butter and brown sugar together in a bowl until smooth. Stir in the eggs. Sift the flour and baking soda together into the bowl and beat until smooth. Add the apples. Fill the prepared ramekins or basins to three-quarters full with the mixture, and set on a baking sheet. Bake in the preheated oven for 25 minutes, or until risen and firm. Let cool for a few minutes, then turn out onto individual dessert plates. Drizzle each cake with a tablespoon of maple syrup and serve immediately with the ice cream.

Spiced Pear Crêpes

Serves 4

Crêpes

2 eggs

1¼ cups milk

**2 tbsp butter, melted, plus
2 tbsp for pan-frying and extra
for greasing**

scant 1 cup all-purpose flour, sifted

pinch of salt

Filling

2 tbsp butter

**2 lb 4 oz/1 kg ripe but firm pears,
peeled, cored, and cut into fairly
large dice**

¼ cup superfine sugar

1 tsp ground cinnamon

1 tsp ground star anise

2 tbsp brandy

scant ⅓ cup golden raisins

**4 pieces preserved ginger,
finely chopped**

4 tbsp preserved ginger syrup

Sauce and Topping

⅔ cup heavy cream

1 tbsp brandy

2 tbsp confectioners' sugar

2 tbsp dark brown sugar

⅓ cup pecans, chopped

sour cream, for serving (optional)

This is a lovely dessert; the crêpes give it a really light touch and it can be made well ahead of time and reheated.

1 To make the crêpes, put the eggs, milk, and melted butter in a food processor or blender and whiz to combine. Mix the flour and salt together, then add to the egg mixture and whiz again until you have a smooth batter. Let stand for 30 minutes–1 hour or longer, if possible.

2 Lightly grease a nonstick skillet or crêpe pan with some of the butter for pan-frying and heat over medium-high heat until hot. Stir the batter, and if it has thickened, add a little water. Pour in a small amount of batter, tilting the pan to spread the mixture over the entire bottom. Add a little more batter if you have any tiny holes. Cook for 1–2 minutes, or until the crêpe is golden on the underside and little bubbles have appeared across the surface. Using a palette knife, gently loosen the crêpe around the edges and turn over. Cook for an additional minute, or until golden brown. Repeat until all the remaining batter is used up—it should make eight crêpes.

3 To make the filling, melt the butter in a large, heavy-bottom skillet over medium heat, then add the pears and cook, stirring frequently, until golden. Add the superfine sugar and spices and continue to cook until the pears are soft. Add the brandy and set alight. When the flames have died down, add the golden raisins, preserved ginger, and ginger syrup. Fill the crêpes with the mixture and roll up. Arrange side by side in a greased flameproof gratin dish.

4 Preheat the broiler to high. For the sauce, lightly whip the cream, brandy, and confectioners' sugar together in a bowl until just beginning to thicken. Pour over the crêpes. Sprinkle over the brown sugar and scatter with the pecans. Cook under the preheated broiler until golden brown and bubbling. Serve immediately with sour cream, if using.

Index